LEITH'S INDIAN AND SRI LANKAN COOKERY

LEITH'S INDIAN AND SRI LANKAN COOKERY

PRIYA WICKRAMASINGHE

FOREWORD BY CAROLINE WALDEGRAVE

PHOTOGRAPHS BY GRAHAM KIRK

BLOOMSBURY

First published in Great Britain in 1997
This paperback edition published in 1998
Bloomsbury Publishing Plc, 38 Soho Square, London W1V 5DF

A CIP catalogue record for this book is available from the British Library

ISBN 0 7475 4197 3

10 9 8 7 6 5 4 3 2 1

Photographer: Graham Kirk
Assisted by: Giovanni Campolo
Stylist: Helen Payne
Home Economist: Puff Fairclough
Assisted by: Jacqui Thomas, Eithne Neane, Philippa Munro, Gina Forshaw

Typeset by Hewer Text Composition Services, Edinburgh
Printed by The Bath Press, Bath

CONTENTS

ACKNOWLEDGEMENTS

I wish to thank in particular the following for their help and advice with recipes: Asma Ali, Lally Chapman, Skol Davies, Medha Dhurandar, Shirani Dayaratne, Mino de Silva, Jayanthi Fernando, Neela Jayawickrema, Koreneris, Shyamala Krishna Swamy, Sandra Lobo, Swarna Moonesinghe, Srimathi Mutucumarana, Mangala Narlikar, Vinitha Rodrigo, Bill Salaman, Uma Sathyaprakash, Iris Senerat-Nandadeva, Duleep Singh and Ranjith Wijeratne. Last but not least, I wish to thank my daughter Kamala for all her hard work, and for the invaluable advice and assistance she has given me throughout the preparation of this volume.

FOREWORD

Priya has been coming to Leith's School to demonstrate Indian cookery for many years. Not only are the students given wonderful recipes and much information on cooking with spices, they also get a real sense of India and Sri Lanka – they begin to understand the history and the culture of the sub-continent. The other thing about Priya is her wonderful charm which she has somehow managed to convey through her recipes and their introductions.

There is a very helpful section on menu-planning and the different styles of food eaten in North and South India. All the recipes one has ever eaten in an Indian restaurant are here plus many more unusual and original ideas. The titles are so inspiring that simply reading them makes one long to make and eat things like Bhindi Thoran, Seeni Sambol and Chole Chaat.

When testing these recipes at the school the smell was wonderful and the enthusiasm for all the dishes enormous. Some of the ingredients obviously need to be bought in specialist shops but for most of the recipes the ingredients can be bought in supermarkets. Indian cookery does not require any exceptional new culinary skills but at the same time you will be justifiably proud when you learn to make successful chapatis and nan breads.

I do hope that you enjoy cooking from this book as much as we have enjoyed working on it.

Caroline Waldegrave

AUTHOR'S PREFACE

This book is the result of a lifelong fascination with Indian and Sri Lankan food. The recipes reflect the experience of my childhood in Sri Lanka and the considerable time I have spent in India gaining first-hand knowledge of Indian cuisine, both in homes and in restaurants.

I am grateful to my many friends in the Indian sub-continent, Sri Lanka, Britain and the USA, who have entertained me in their homes and inspired some of the recipes in this book. I also wish to thank my family for all the support and encouragement they gave me during what seemed like an unending period of testing, tasting and writing. I am especially grateful to my daughter Kamala for writing the introduction and the preface to the spice index, as well as for extensive editorial help.

I would also like to thank the staff at Leith's School for their heroic effort in testing each and every recipe, C.J. for arranging the testing, Puff for organizing the photographs and Caroline for her support throughout the project.

Here's to currying flavours!

Priya Wickramasinghe
Cardiff
March 1997

CONVERSION TABLES

The tables below are approximate, and do not conform in all respects to the conventional conversions, but we have found them convenient for cooking. Use either metric or imperial measurements. But do not mix the two.

Weight

Imperial	Metric	Imperial	Metric
¼oz	7–8g	½oz	15g
¾oz	20g	1oz	30g
2oz	55g	3oz	85g
4oz (¼lb)	110g	5oz	140g
6oz	170g	7oz	200g
8oz (½lb)	225g	9oz	255g
10oz	285g	11oz	310g
12oz (¾lb)	340g	13oz	370g
14oz	400g	15oz	425g
16oz (1lb)	450g	1¼lb	560g
1½lb	675g	2lb	900g
3lb	1.35kg	4lb	1.8kg
5lb	2.3kg	6lb	2.7kg
7lb	3.2kg	8lb	3.6kg
9lb	4.0kg	10lb	4.5kg

Australian cup measures

	Metric	Imperial
1 cup flour	140g	5oz
1 cup sugar (crystal or caster)	225g	8oz
1 cup brown sugar, firmly packed	170g	6oz
1 cup icing sugar, sifted	170g	6oz
1 cup butter	225g	8oz
1 cup honey, golden syrup, treacle	370g	12oz
1 cup fresh breadcrumbs	55g	2oz
1 cup packaged dry breadcrumbs	140g	5oz
1 cup crushed biscuit crumbs	110g	4oz
1 cup rice, uncooked	200g	7oz
1 cup mixed fruit or individual fruit, such as sultanas	170g	6oz
1 cup nuts, chopped	110g	4oz
1 cup coconut, desiccated	85g	3oz

Approximate American/European conversions

	USA	Metric	Imperial
Flour	1 cup	140g	5oz
Caster and granulated sugar	1 cup	225g	8oz
Caster and granulated sugar	2 level tablespoons	30g	1oz
Brown sugar	1 cup	170g	6oz
Butter/margarine/lard	1 cup	225g	8oz
Sultanas/raisins	1 cup	200g	7oz
Currants	1 cup	140g	5oz
Ground almonds	1 cup	110g	4oz
Golden syrup	1 cup	340g	12oz
Uncooked rice	1 cup	200g	7oz
Grated cheese	1 cup	110g	4oz
Butter	1 stick	110g	4oz

Liquid measures

Imperial	ml	fl oz
1 teaspoon	5	
2 scant tablespoons	28	
4 scant tablespoons	56	
¼ pint (1 gill)	150	5
⅓ pint	190	6.6
½ pint	290	10
¾ pint	425	15
1 pint	570	20
1¾ pints	1000 (1 litre)	35

Australian

250ml	1 cup
20ml	1 tablespoon
5ml	1 teaspoon

Approximate American/European conversions

American	European
1 teaspoon	1 teaspoon/5ml
½fl oz	1 tablespoon/½fl oz/15ml
¼ cup	4 tablespoons/2fl oz/55ml
½ cup plus 2 tablespoons	¼ pint/5fl oz/150ml
1¼ cups	½ pint/10fl oz/290ml
1 pint/16fl oz	1 pint/20fl oz/570ml
2½ pints (5 cups)	1.1 litres/2 pints
10 pints	4.5 litres/8 pints

Useful measurements

Measurement	Metric	Imperial
1 American cup	225ml	8fl oz
1 egg, size 3	56ml	2fl oz
1 egg white	28ml	1fl oz
1 rounded tablespoon flour	30g	1oz
1 rounded tablespoon cornflour	30g	1oz
1 rounded tablespoon caster sugar	30g	1oz
2 rounded tablespoons fresh breadcrumbs	30g	1oz
2 level teaspoons gelatine	8g	¼oz

30g/1oz granular (packet) aspic sets 570ml/1 pint liquid.

15g/½oz powdered gelatine, or 3 leaves, will set 570ml/1 pint liquid. (However, in hot weather, or if the liquid is very acid, like lemon juice, or if the jelly contains solid pieces of fruit and is to be turned out of the dish or mould, 20g/¾oz should be used.)

Wine quantities

Imperial	ml	fl oz
Average wine bottle	750	25
1 glass wine	100	3
1 glass port or sherry	70	2
1 glass liqueur	45	1

Lengths

Imperial	Metric
½in	1cm
1in	2.5cm
2in	5cm
6in	15cm
12in	30cm

Oven temperatures

<table>
<tr><th>°C</th><th>°F</th><th>Gas mark</th><th>AMERICAN</th><th>AUSTRALIAN</th></tr>
<tr><td>70</td><td>150</td><td>¼</td><td rowspan="4">COOL</td><td rowspan="5">VERY SLOW</td></tr>
<tr><td>80</td><td>175</td><td>¼</td></tr>
<tr><td>100</td><td>200</td><td>½</td></tr>
<tr><td>110</td><td>225</td><td>½</td></tr>
<tr><td>130</td><td>250</td><td>1</td><td rowspan="2">VERY SLOW</td></tr>
<tr><td>140</td><td>275</td><td>1</td><td rowspan="2">SLOW</td></tr>
<tr><td>150</td><td>300</td><td>2</td><td>SLOW</td></tr>
<tr><td>170</td><td>325</td><td>3</td><td rowspan="2">MODERATE</td><td rowspan="2">MODERATELY SLOW</td></tr>
<tr><td>180</td><td>350</td><td>4</td></tr>
<tr><td>190</td><td>375</td><td>5</td><td>MODERATELY HOT</td><td rowspan="2">MODERATE</td></tr>
<tr><td>200</td><td>400</td><td>6</td><td>FAIRLY HOT</td></tr>
<tr><td>220</td><td>425</td><td>7</td><td>HOT</td><td rowspan="2">MODERATELY HOT</td></tr>
<tr><td>230</td><td>450</td><td>8</td><td rowspan="2">VERY HOT</td></tr>
<tr><td>240</td><td>475</td><td>8</td><td rowspan="2">HOT</td></tr>
<tr><td>250</td><td>500</td><td>9</td><td rowspan="3">EXTREMELY HOT</td></tr>
<tr><td>270</td><td>525</td><td>9</td><td rowspan="2">VERY HOT</td></tr>
<tr><td>290</td><td>550</td><td>9</td></tr>
</table>

INTRODUCTION

Today mouth-watering images of Indian food – curries, baltis, tandooris – greet us at every street corner. In London alone there are well over 1000 Indian restaurants, with ambitious new eating houses springing up every other week across the nation. Supermarkets stock complete ready-made Indian meals, and chicken tikka sandwiches are a huge-selling lunchtime favourite. The present-day popularity of Indian food is unequivocal. However, it is only the scale of this 'spice explosion' that is a recent phenomenon. A taste for Indian food has existed in Britain since the eighteenth century as one of the legacies of colonial times. The British who were posted for various assignments inevitably acquired a lasting addiction to Indian food. When they returned home they brought back recipes for curries, mulligatawny and chutneys, which were adapted and eventually assimilated into English cuisine. Queen Victoria is reputed to have had two Indian cooks, a rumour which testifies to a long-standing desire for exotic food. One way or another, the British palate became accustomed to the taste of chillies, ginger and spices. And at the beginning of the twentieth century, the first Indian restaurants were starting to emerge in London.

To appreciate Indian and Sri Lankan food fully one really has to taste and see it in context. The food does, of course, stand in its own right, offering a delicious variety of taste sensations. But it is greatly enhanced by an understanding of its relation to a cultural and religious backdrop. The vast majority of chefs at Indian restaurants in Britain hail from a particular part of the province of Bengal: the Sylhet region. Even though the indigenous food of Bengal is undoubtedly specialized, the menus rarely highlight this regional aspect. On the contrary, restaurateurs have been enterprising enough to stretch their range of products to include diverse cuisines, even to the extent of inventing menu combinations that may be considered unorthodox. Such menus have regrettably often been adapted to suit the anglicized palate. Most patrons of Indian restaurants in Britain expect meat to form an essential component of their menu, and this expectation is not compromised. Traditional vegetarian and non-vegetarian dishes are often mixed indiscriminately, and the food served in such restaurants bears little or no resemblance to what one would be served in India.

The preparation of authentic dishes is a central concern of this book, but what also emerges as important is a discovery of why the food is prepared and served in the way it is. The food of India is the result of the synthesis of land and climate with the religious, social and cultural life of the people who live there. All major world religions have a strong presence in the sub-continent, although the Hindus and Moslems are the most numerous. The Hindu veneration of the cow has led to beef taboos as well as a variety of vegetarian traditions, the most austere of which are to be found amongst the Brahmin (priest caste) Tamils of South India and Sri Lanka. The Moslems, on the other hand, when they do not fast, indulge their senses more lavishly; although they shun pork as part of a religious taboo, they consume a variety of other meats prepared in the most exotic ways. The Seikhs, however, eat pork; and the Buddhists of Sri Lanka, though vegetarian in their more austere practice, avoid meat but do eat fish. It goes without saying that every single religious group in India has its own distinctive food style. Not only do they have their own particular food taboos, they have their celebratory dishes as well. It is precisely this diversity of religious and cultural traditions that has contributed to the richness and variety that is to be found in Indian food. The culinary differences between different regions of India are at least as great as those between, say, France and Germany.

Despite its proximity to India, Sri Lanka cannot be considered simply as an extension of the neighbouring sub-continent. Culturally, geographically, climatically and indeed gastronomically, the differences are marked, although of course connecting threads to southern Indian regions do exist. The links with Kerala are particularly strong in regard to preparations such as *aappam* and *indiaappam* (hoppers and string hoppers), and there are surviving culinary links with Sri Lanka's rich colonial history. Perhaps the most distinctive nature of Sri Lankan food is the use of Maldive fish (dried fish) which is added as a flavour-enhancer to vegetable dishes. Coconut and chilli also form an integral part of most Sri Lankan dishes.

Throughout India and Sri Lanka, European conquests have also influenced food habits and culinary styles. Many a hybrid dish has been invented in this way, often combining indigenous spices with culinary traditions of the West. For instance, in Goa a distinctly Portuguese influence is seen in the variety of pork dishes. The standard Goan sausage is a variation of the Spanish/Portuguese chorizo, a long, coiled-up red sausage that is sometimes curried. The Portuguese liking for sweetened egg-yolk preparations is also seen in the Goan celebratory cake known as *bibican*, which combines coconut, egg and sugar. There is also a Sri Lankan version of *bibikkan* (see page **221**) as Sri Lanka was a Portuguese colony before it fell into the hands of the Dutch and then the British.

Across the vast Indian sub-continent, from Northern India, Bangladesh and

Pakistan to Sri Lanka in the south, the variations of climate and terrain are dramatic. A large part of this land mass is fertile and produces a wide range of crops. An innumerable variety of vegetables is found, ranging from distinctly tropical vegetables to those that grow in temperate climates. Vegetable dishes prepared in a multitude of exciting ways form the major part of the Eastern diet. Meat and fish are for the most part a luxury, eaten by a comparatively affluent minority. Rice is the staple food in Bengal, Southern India and Sri Lanka, whereas wheat is the staple food in the North. The spices which give Indian food its distinctive flavour and character are grown throughout the entire sub-continent. Not only are the types of spices important in preparing particular dishes, the blending of one spice with another is equally important and produces subtle differences in flavour.

This book is not just another compendium of Indian recipes which simply tells you how to re-create the most popular dishes served in Indian restaurants. The authentic dishes presented here cover an enormous range of delicacies which you might taste if you were to travel the length and breadth of India. The recipes, along with introductions that place them in context, reflect the author's personal experience of Sri Lankan and Indian food over a lifetime.

SPECIAL INGREDIENTS

SPICES

Spices from the East have been a much-sought-after commodity from the earliest historical times, and desire for the monopoly of spice routes has caused almost as many wars as has religion.

In the Bible there are numerous references to the high value that was placed on spices. Such was their worth that they could be used as currency in bribes: the Queen of Sheba rushed to present Solomon with gold, jewels and spices when she feared that an alliance with his Phoenician neighbours would threaten the trade routes she controlled (Kings I:10 and Chronicles II:9).

As early as 1700 BC Egypt was importing spices from India to use for embalming mummies. For many centuries, the overland trade routes to India and South-East Asia were controlled by Arab merchants. Shrewd middlemen used to invent fantastical stories about the difficulty of procuring spices in order to fleece their Western buyers. They said that the mountains of Arabia were inhabited by monstrous birds which made their nests out of cinnamon twigs, far from the reach of humans. These birds had a liking for donkey meat, so natives used to leave hefty chunks of it lying about. The birds would fly their booty back to their nests which collapsed under the weight. The ingenious Arabs would be waiting below to collect the cinnamon!

The Middle Eastern monopoly came to an end in the first century AD when the Romans discovered how to work the sea routes to India with the aid of the monsoon winds. The journey which had taken two years by land now took less than a year, and the Romans became extravagant users of spices for cooking, medicine, perfume and cosmetics. Their love of peppers was so great that in Sanskrit the new word for pepper was *Yavanpriya*, meaning 'dear to the European'. This era of trade between East and West came to an end with the fall of the Roman Empire, the growth of Islam and the chaos of the Dark Ages.

Trade with the East was reopened by the Crusades in the eleventh century, and after bitter fighting between Italian city states, the Venetians took control of the spice trade. They charged such exorbitant prices, however, that the Portuguese tried to find their own supplies and discovered that they could reach India by sailing past Africa.

The history of India and Sri Lanka was intimately connected with the desire of Western nations to secure control of the spice trade. During the sixteenth century, the Portuguese established a colonial grip on the spice-producing areas of the East. Their dominance ended in the seventeenth century when they were driven out by the Dutch, who, in turn, were driven out by the British in the eighteenth century.

In the East, spices have always had a variety of uses. They are valued not only as condiments, but also for their medicinal and health-giving properties. Clove oil is used as an anaesthetic, turmeric as an antiseptic and fennel as a digestive, to name but a few. In Sri Lanka, a brew of whole dry-roasted coriander seeds, ginger and sugar is used as a remedy for colds. Even dandruff may be treated by a home-made shampoo consisting of boiled fenugreek and lime.

Most of the spices that are used in Eastern cuisine are readily available in Indian and Chinese supermarkets and even in some of the larger supermarket chains. There is a dearth of adjectives in the English language to describe the subtle differences in flavour that are produced by blending together various combinations of spices. The commonly used 'pungent' and 'aromatic' have too broad an application and the palate is privileged in being able to experience more than the tongue can express. Listed below are a number of spices and a few other commodities used in Indian and Sri Lankan cooking.

Amchoor: This is the name given to a dried mango powder which is used to flavour vegetable dishes. It is available in specialist stores.

Aniseed: This spice is widely grown throughout Asia and is used in curries in a roasted form. It is a seed derived from the herb *Pimpinella anisum.*

Asafoetida: This pungent-smelling resin is obtained from the root of the herb *Ferula foetida.* It is cultivated widely in the Middle East and is used in many vegetable dishes.

Capsicum: This is a sweet pepper, used for curries. It is not hot or pungent like chilli.

Cardamom: These are the dried seeds of *Elettaria cardamomum*, a herb of the ginger family. Whole cardamom pods are used for flavouring rice, but should be removed before serving. For curries the seeds are removed from the pods and ground. In some parts of India cardamoms are used for flavouring tea and coffee. Cardamom pods are also chewed after meals as a breath-sweetener.

Cayenne pepper: This is made by grinding the dried pods and seeds of *Capsicum frutescens* to a fine powder. It is darker than paprika and very much hotter. Cayenne pepper is a good substitute for chilli.

Chilli: This is a hot variety of capsicum and can be either red or green. There are about 200 varieties of chilli which are grown in all parts of the world. As a general rule, the smaller the chilli the hotter it is. The hotness of the chilli comes from the chemical capsaicin which is mainly in the seeds and veins, so de-seeded chillies can be used to enhance flavour without giving heat. Dried red chilli pods are ground to make chilli powder which is used to spice curries, as are whole dried and fresh chillies.

Recent medical research has suggested that eating chillies could produce the same feel-good factor that exercise fanatics become hooked on. Scientists have claimed that endorphins, the body's morphine-like painkillers, are released into our brain when we bite into chilli peppers.

Chillies have a practical use in hot climates as hotness makes people perspire, which lowers the body temperature. In India, as you travel further south, both the climate and the curries become increasingly hotter, and by the time you reach Sri Lanka they are dynamite! After handling chillies, particularly the seeds, extreme care should be taken not to touch any sensitive part of the body as this causes a burning sensation.

Cinnamon: This fragrant spice is the dried bark of *Cinnamomum zeylanicum*, grown mainly in Sri Lanka. It is an important ingredient of curries, and is also used in sweet dishes.

Cloves: These dried unopened flower-buds of *Eugenia caryophyllata* or *Myrtus caryophyllus* are another major ingredient in Indian and Sri Lankan cooking. Cloves were an important commodity in the spice trade.

Coriander: The leaves of *Coriandrum sativum* are used for garnishing, and the crushed seeds are used in curry powder.

Creamed coconut: This is the milk extracted from the grated kernel of the coconut, the fruit of the palm *Cocos nucifera*, which grows abundantly throughout the coastal regions of South-East Asia. It is readily available in the form of solid blocks from most good grocery stores. See coconut (page **14**).

Cumin: The seeds of black cumin (*Cuminum nigrum*) and white cumin (*Cuminum cyminum*) are ground and used in many savoury and some sweet dishes.

Curry leaves: The leaves of *Murraya koenigii*, a small shrub of the orange family, are often used in curries, particularly in South India and Sri Lanka. They add a characteristic fragrance and flavour.

Fennel: This herb is thought to be one of the oldest used by man. Ground seeds of *Foeniculum vulgare* or *Nigella sativa* are used in curries. Fresh and dried seeds are also chewed after a meal as a digestive aid and breath-sweetener.

Fenugreek: This spice is derived from the aromatic seeds of the plant *Trigonella foenicum graecum*. Roasted, ground fenugreek seeds are used in curry powder.

Gamboge: The bright orange-coloured segmented fruit from trees of the genus *Garcinia*. A delicious drink can be made from fresh segments. When they are dry, the segments become black in colour and are kidney shaped. Because gamboge has a high acid content it acts as a preservative.

Garam masala: This is the name given to any mixture of spices used for curries. Commercially mixed garam masala is available in supermarkets. Recipes for making your own garam masala from individual spices are given on page **31**.

Ginger: This is the root of the herbaceous plant *Zingiber officinalis* which is used extensively in Indian and Sri Lankan cooking. Fresh ginger (called 'green ginger') is to be preferred to dried ginger powder.

Gram flour/Lentil flour: This is a flour made from chana dhal and is used in both sweet and savoury dishes. It is readily available from Indian shops where it is known as *besan*.

Jaggery: This sweetening agent, obtained from various types of palm, is used for making many Sri Lankan desserts. It is an unrefined brown sugar made mainly from the sap of the toddy palm (*Caryota urens*). It is available in Sri Lankan shops in a ready-to-use form known as Kitul treacle. Indian jaggery is lighter in colour than Sri Lankan and is made from cane sugar. For the recipes in this book only Sri Lankan jaggery should be used.

Lentil: Cultivated Eurasian annual plant (*Lens culinaris*). Its flattened seeds are cooked like peas or beans and are also ground into flour. Lentils are sometimes split and husked. There are many varieties of lentils, and it is regarded as being the 'poor man's meat' in South-East Asia. It is the main source of protein for vegetarians. Chana, Urad, Thur, split mung beans and orange lentils are different varieties of lentils. Thur dhal is yellow in colour and takes a longer time to cook than most other varieties. Unhusked urad dhal is black, and the husked split lentil is creamy white. Chana is also a yellow-coloured lentil used especially for lentil rissoles (Vade, see page **183**).

Mace: The lacy outer covering of nutmeg (see below).

Maldive fish: Dried fish from the Maldive Islands is used in many Sri Lankan curries. It is sold in specialist grocery stores.

Mustard seed: The small dark-brown seed of *Brassica juncea* is used whole and fried in hot oil in the preparation of most curries. Mustard oil is also used in cooking, particularly in Bengal.

Nutmeg: The seed of the evergreen tree *Myristica fragrans*. Grated nutmeg is used in both curries and sweet dishes. Nutmeg is grown in Sri Lanka and throughout the Malay archipelago.

Paprika: Made from dried, finely-ground pods of various sweet peppers (of the pimento family). Although not generally used in Asian cooking, I use it as a substitute for chilli powder, as it gives a dish a red colour without the heat of chillies.

Pepper: Piper nigrum, the most familiar of spices, comes from a vine native to Sri Lanka, South India and Malaya. Dried berries become peppercorns, which can be ground.

Poppy seeds: Seeds of the opium poppy (*Papaver somniferum*) are often added to curry powders. They have no smell, but have a nutty flavour. They are believed to stimulate the appetite.

Rice sticks: Fine vermicelli made of rice flour, available in Chinese and Indian supermarkets.

Saffron: The dried stamen of *Crocus sativus* is one of the most expensive of spices. Saffron gives a delicate aroma and a golden-yellow colour.

Screwpine: The tropical tree *Pandanus odoratissimus*. The shiny green-pointed leaves of the screwpine are referred to as *rampe* in Sri Lanka, and are used in curries and in rice dishes. Fresh screwpine leaves can be kept for about a week in the refrigerator. Dried screwpine, which has less flavour, may be stored in airtight containers. It is available in oriental food stores, including Sri Lankan shops.

Sesame seeds: Seeds from the herbaceous plant *Sesamum indicum* are used extensively in Indian cooking. The seeds are used in sweets. Oil from the seed is called gingerly oil and is used for frying. The powdered seeds are often mixed into curry powders. Sesame seeds are considered to be a mild laxative.

Tamarind: The dried fruit of the tamarind tree (*Tamarindus indica*) can be soaked in hot water to extract its tart acidic juice. This extract is then used for preparing curry dishes. Instant tamarind extract is now readily available.

Turmeric: The root of *Curcuma longa*, a perennial herb related to the ginger family, is dried and then ground into a brilliant yellow-coloured powder, used for flavouring and colouring curries.

Cinnamon, cardamom, cumin, nutmeg, clove, fennel, coriander, turmeric and chilli are cultivated extensively throughout the Indian sub-continent and Sri Lanka, and these are the main flavouring ingredients of a curry. To make curry powder all these spices are ground and mixed together in varying proportions. Every region in India and Sri Lanka has its own special curry powder – Bafath powder from Goa, a black spice powder from Maharashtra, Goda masala, five-spice powder from Bengal, and yet another type of special curry powder from Sri Lanka called *thuna paha* (three-plus-five-spice powder).

COCONUT

Coconuts, the fruit of the *Cocos nucifera* tree, which belongs to the palm family, represents one of the most important crops of the tropics. Fruits take a whole year to ripen. A coconut fruit consists of a fibrous outer skin, a hard inner shell and an interior comprised of white 'flesh' or kernel and a clear liquid.

Coconut milk: This is not the water inside the coconut, but a milky liquid that is extracted from the grated kernel. In Britain it is available in three ready-to-use forms: creamed coconut, coconut milk powder and coconut milk. Creamed coconut is solidified coconut milk and has to be dissolved in hot water. Coconut milk powder also needs to be made up with water, but canned coconut milk is ready to use.

The traditional way to prepare coconut milk in India and Sri Lanka is to start with a fresh coconut. When buying a fresh coconut, always shake it to ensure that it is full of liquid. If it sounds hollow it is invariably old! Pierce two of the three eyes (the circular indentations in the coconut) and drain off the coconut water. (In Sri Lanka the coconut water from tender young coconuts is chilled and used as a refreshing drink.) Next, break the coconut by hitting it very hard with a hammer on a strong paving stone. If it is difficult to crack the coconut put it into the oven at 150°C/300°F/gas mark 2 for 15 minutes. It should crack on its own as it cools, or it can be cracked with a slight tap of a hammer. Prise out the flesh, peel off the brown outer skin and grate, either in a food processor or with a hand-held grater (see page **20**). A very small amount of hot water is now added to the grated coconut and the liquid is extracted by forcing through a sieve. This liquid from the 'first press' is referred to as 'thick' coconut milk. The process can be repeated by adding hot water again to the same grated coconut and straining; the resulting liquid from the second press is thinner and is referred to as 'thin' coconut milk. In India and Sri Lanka special equipment is available both for grating and breaking the nut.

RICE

Because the staple food of a large part of India and Sri Lanka is rice, a rice dish is invariably included in a menu plan (see pages **237–8**). Fish, meat and vegetable curries and salads are arranged, often artistically, around a main rice dish.

Rice, which belongs to the grass family, is native to South-East Asia. It has been cultivated for over 7000 years and still constitutes the main food of over half the world's population. Rice is now cultivated in most countries of South and East Asia, Egypt, Southern Europe, Southern United States and Brazil. Over half a billion tonnes of rice were harvested in 1996, with China in the lead, contributing 36 per cent of the total, and India in second place, contributing 26 per cent.

There are many varieties of rice. The

most popular varieties marketed in Britain are American long-grain rice (Uncle Ben's rice is well known) and basmati rice, grown in India and Pakistan.

Less common is the glutinous round-grain rice which is grown mostly in Japan. This is best suited for Japanese and Chinese cuisine, whilst arborio rice, grown in the Po valley of southern Italy, is the best variety for risotto dishes. The best rice for Indian cooking is basmati rice which is grown in the river deltas of Northern India, but patna rice, which is also a long-grain rice, is much cheaper and suitable for most of the dishes in this book. In Sri Lanka country rice or red rice, which is only slightly polished and retains much of the rice bran, is popular in rural districts. The bran has a high nutritional content, containing vitamins B complex, E and K. Fully polished white rice is less nutritious, containing about 25 per cent starch and small amounts of iodine, iron, magnesium and phosphorus.
However, for special Sri Lankan dishes such as Yellow Rice (see page **40**), a pearly white polished rice called Samba is used.

Throughout most of Asia rice is treated with the respect and veneration it deserves. The dictum in Sri Lanka is that to throw away rice is a sin. Rice grain is never wasted, nor even used as feed for farm animals. One never sits on a sack of rice, no matter how tired one might be!

In many parts of the Indian sub-continent rice has come to be synonymous with food and sustenance. For example, in Sri Lanka the question 'Have you had lunch?' is phrased as 'Have you eaten rice?'

COOKING RICE

There is no mystique about cooking rice. A measured quantity of rice grain is first washed in a sieve under running cold water to wash away the loose starch. By far the most popular method of cooking rice is the 'absorption method' where a measure of rice (a cup is a convenient measure) is mixed with approximately a measure and a half of water in a saucepan and boiled, covered tightly, for exactly 15 minutes (see page **37**). All the water should be absorbed into the rice grains, and the rice properly cooked with the grains remaining separate. Traditionally no salt is added to the rice, because its purity of taste acts as a palate-cleanser.

A quaint custom in Sri Lanka is the 'finger method' of measuring the water required for the rice. The washed rice is put in a cooking pot and just enough water added so that the height of the water level over the surface of the rice is exactly two phalanges of an index finger (approximately 5cm/2in). This always seems to work, irrespective of the size of the pan. If all else fails there is an electric rice cooker on the market which not only cooks the rice but keeps it warm until needed.

COOKING EQUIPMENT AND UTENSILS

As in all forms of indigenous cooking throughout the world, the utensils and equipment used have an intimate connection with the place and people concerned. India has a civilization stretching back over several thousand years, and Indian cooking has of necessity evolved over this long period of history. Today, Indian cooking can be seen to reflect the interplay between many ancient (and not so ancient!) cultures. Against a truly indigenous background of Vedhic Aryan tradition one can clearly discern the more recent intermingling of Mogul and European influences. All these hybrid influences have contributed to make for rich variety in Indian and Sri Lankan food.

The very earliest cooking utensils and equipment excavated from numerous archaeological sites give an interesting insight into the primitive beginnings of Indian culinary skills. Fragments of clay ovens, clay pots and iron skewers have all been found, some in the very oldest cities of the Indus Valley civilization, including the famous ruined city of Moenjodaro. Some of this apparatus bears a strikingly close similarity to pots and stoves in present-day use, so one may safely infer that the basic traditions of Indian cookery became established a very long time ago.

Throughout most of India and Sri Lanka, in remote villages as well as on the streets of bustling modern cities, the cooking equipment to be seen is invariably of a primitive, traditional kind. Cooking is often done over an open coal or firewood stove built of bricks and clay in a seemingly makeshift fashion. The clay oven known as the *tandoor* is a common sight throughout much of Northern India, along with many other types of traditional utensils. Traditional grinding stones and cooking pots such as the clay *chattie*, *degchi*, *katchari* and *tava* are frequently seen.

It would of course be unfair to say that Indian and Sri Lankan cooking has not benefited from or been influenced by the advent of Western devices and utensils, particularly the gas hob and modern electric ovens. Indeed, most city chefs in both homes and hotels tend to take advantage of modern appliances and utensils, whether as improvisations or short-cuts. Inevitably the Indian cook in the West (to whom this book is directed) will be forced to improvise and to use what is readily at hand. In this section I shall describe most of the important items of traditional cooking equipment, indicate for what purposes they are used, and make suggestions for replacement or substitution in the context of the Western kitchen. It will be seen that there is no major problem in the conversion or adaptation of a standard Western kitchen to cope with most forms of Indian cooking.

UTENSILS FOR PREPARATION

The preparation of ingredients for cooking is a matter of great importance in Indian and Sri Lankan cooking.

GRINDING/BLENDING EQUIPMENT

Spices need to be ground into a fine powder and mixed prior to use; grain needs to be ground into flour; and often a variety of ingredients need to be ground with liquid to form a smooth paste. The traditional chef has several appliances to help in these varied tasks. Most widely used is the stone mortar and pestle, of which there are several types. Another device used for much the same purpose is the grinding stone. This is used for pounding grain or for mixing ingredients to form a paste. A mortar and pestle is a feasible import into the Western kitchen and one that I strongly recommend. However, most of the grinding and blending required in Indian cooking is now most conveniently done using an electric grinder, a blender or a food processor.

SIFTING/SIEVING EQUIPMENT

Several items of equipment are traditionally used for separating stray stones and husks from rice and pulses. The *nambiliya* is a hemispherical aluminium pot with parallel circular grooves. Rice or pulses containing sand or stones are washed in water in the *nambiliya* and the mixture given a rapid rotary motion so that the particles of sand or stone are centrifuged out to become trapped in the grooves. The grain can then be easily separated from the unwanted stone.

The loose husk of grain is removed by winnowing, using a shallow, closely woven wicker basket. The mixture of husk and grain is repeatedly jerked upwards in a skilful movement that effectively throws out the husk and collects the grain back in the wicker basket. This implement is also used to sieve out the coarser lumps from any form of ground flour. Most of the traditional uses of such sifting/sieving equipment are now made superfluous by the ready-sifted, ready-cleaned ingredients available in the Western market. However, a large plastic or metal sieve is most useful for many purposes and is to be recommended as part of the equipment for a Western Indian kitchen.

GRATING EQUIPMENT

There are several types of traditional equipment used for grating. The most specialized of these is the coconut grater, a device known as the *hiramane*, used for scraping out the kernel of the coconut (see page **14**), which can be obtained from specialist Indian shops. The grating attachment of a food processor could be usefully deployed to perform the same function, but the coconut kernel must first be scooped clear of the shell. Other traditional grating devices are all easily replaced by a simple metal grater that can be bought in any supermarket.

PASTRY-MAKING UTENSILS

Rolling out pastry and dough forms an important preparation for many types of Indian bread. The *chakla-belan* is a flat, circular wooden board together with a wooden rolling pin that is fat in the middle and tapers at the ends. If you cannot find a *chakla-belan*, an ordinary wooden pastry board and wooden rolling pin will suffice.

CHOPPING UTENSILS

Chopping, slicing and dicing ingredients need to be done quite frequently in the preparation of Indian and Sri Lankan food. The traditional equipment is no more, no less than a large flat wooden board kept aside for this purpose, together with a selection of very sharp knives.

THE PRESS

A two-piece hand-held wooden press which works on the piston principle is used to squeeze out batter into vermicelli-like threads. Metal discs with perforations of various designs can be inserted at the base of the press to get threads with attractive shapes. An icing bag with different-shaped nozzles would provide a convenient substitute in most cases.

UTENSILS FOR COOKING

POTS AND PANS

Clay pots known as *chatties* are amongst the most ancient utensils used in Indian and Sri Lankan cooking. Such pots conduct heat slowly and evenly, which is ideal for slow cooking and simmering. Clay has the property of retaining heat from the fire, which is very useful if the heat source fluctuates in strength. Clay pots take on a flavour of their own, so different pots must be kept for meat, fish and vegetable cooking. Earthenware casserole pots are now readily available in the West and may be used to advantage in preparations such as biriyanis and pilafs. If this is impractical, heavy metal saucepans with heavy lids will do. A heavy metal saucepan has some of the desirable properties of a *chattie* in that the heat is distributed over the inside surface fairly evenly. In modern India the *chattie* has come to be at least partially replaced by heavy brassware, aluminium ware, and more recently by heavy stainless-steel pans.

The brass *degchi* has come to be used as a traditional substitute for the more primitive *chattie*. It is essentially a saucepan without handles, with a flat lid that can fit tightly over the rim of the pan, and is sometimes sealed down by means of a flour–water paste. The *degchi* is a versatile receptacle with many uses, for example as an oven when hot coals are placed on top of the flat lid as well as in the base.

The *karhai* is the Indian version of the Chinese wok, made of iron, brass, aluminium or stainless steel. It is deep and curved at the bottom, with a pair of handles on diametrically opposite points of the rim. It is used for deep-frying or stir-frying. A Chinese wok is a perfectly good substitute.

The *tava* is used traditionally for grilling chapatis, parathas and other Indian breads. It is a circular-shaped, heavy cast-iron plate that is placed over hot coals. A suitable replacement would be an iron griddle or even a large, heavy-based frying pan.

SPOONS AND TONGS

A pair of long metal tongs, the *cheemta*, is often used to turn over chapatis on a hot griddle. It is also used for holding papadams to be roasted over coals, or even to turn over live coals. An ordinary pair of iron tongs with a long handle and blunt ends would suffice to replace this traditional item.

A flat spoon with a long handle (the *karchchi*) comes in very handy for pressing and holding down discs of dough or papadams on to a hot griddle. A round flat frying spoon would do the job just as well.

A perforated metal spoon with a long handle, called the *janna*, is used to make drops of batter for pouring into hot oil. A similar effect can be obtained by the careful use of a small ladle or spoon.

A coconut shell spoon consists of a cleaned-out half coconut shell with a long wooden stick attached to it as a handle. This is often used for stirring the contents of a pot while it cooks. A straightforward replacement would be an ordinary wooden spoon or ladle.

SKEWERS

Cubes of meat are strung on to long, thin, circular metal skewers known as *seekhs*, to be grilled over hot coals. Minced meat with various added ingredients is also wrapped round similar skewers and grilled. The skewers used for barbecues are an entirely suitable replacement for the *seekh*.

STOVES AND OVENS

The cooking stoves traditionally used in India are exceedingly primitive. The *chulha* is a roughly semi-circular hearth built of brick and clay under which the fuel is burned. The fuel of choice is either firewood or charcoal. This type of traditional fireplace is coming to be replaced to an increasing extent by gas and electric stoves.

The *tandoor* is perhaps the most famous of the indigenous Indian ovens. It is in essence a large dugout pit with baked clay walls into which live coals are piled at the base. Bread (nan) is slapped on to the walls of the pit, and meat and chicken threaded on long skewers are thrown in for baking above the coals. This is a very ancient method of Indian cooking and one that is still quite extensively used in the North.

SPECIALIZED UTENSILS

In addition to the utensils mentioned above, there are several highly specialized items of equipment used for steaming a variety of preparations made of rice and lentil flour. Unfortuately, such equipment cannot be substituted and it is for this reason that I have had to omit delicacies such as *idli* (steamed lentil and rice flour savoury snack), *pittu* (steamed rice flour and coconut bread) and *appam* (fermented crispy pancake with a crumpet-like centre). To make *idli* you need an idli steamer, which is similar to an egg poacher but has fine perforations at the base of each cup into which the batter is poured. For steaming *pittu* bamboo tubes are required and for steaming *indiappam* wicker racks are used. *Appam* (also known as hoppers) are cooked in small hemispherical pans resembling tiny woks.

COOKING TECHNIQUES

BROWNING CHOPPED ONIONS

In certain recipes, finely chopped onions need to be fried until golden-brown. The onions must first be chopped very finely and evenly. If the pieces of onion are of varying size the smaller pieces will burn before the bigger ones are browned.

When frying onions the oil temperature is critical. The onions have to be fried over a low to medium heat and should be stirred from time to time. Always remember that an appropriate quantity of oil has to be used. Although quantities of oil have been specified in the recipes, remember to use your judgement, as the amount of oil needed will be dependent on the size of pan you use. There is also a critical point between browning onions and burning them that has to be recognized!

DEEP-FRYING

For deep-frying it is essential to use enough oil to submerge the item you are frying. Remember that the oil temperature drops the moment any food item is added to the pan of hot oil. Therefore only deep-fry a few items at a time and always bring the oil back to the correct temperature before each new addition.

In order to retain the crispness of anything deep-fried, I first use a cooling rack to drain off most of the oil. Then I use kitchen paper to finish off the draining. I picked up this technique in Japan, when I watched my friends make tempura.

DEEP-FRIED ONIONS

These are always used as a garnish. Supermarkets now stock deep-fried onion flakes in sealed containers, and I have found that it is easy to make your own by using dried onion flakes. Remember that onion flakes are very light and only take a second or two to burn. Since they expand in the hot oil, only a very small quantity should be fried at a time. Always drain off the excess oil on kitchen paper and store in an airtight container for up to a week. Of course freshly sliced onions can be deep-fried too. They require a lot more time to brown, however, and hence more effort.

WHOLE SPICES IN HOT OIL

Each region of India and Sri Lanka has a specific word for this unique Eastern technique where whole spices are added to hot oil and left to pop or sizzle. Care should be taken to heat the oil over a low to medium heat – if the oil temperature is too high the curries made using the spices will be bitter.

It is normal to 'pop' mustard seeds in the oil before frying onions and adding ground spices. When frying spices in oil, not only do you bring out the flavour of the spices, you also distribute the flavour into the oil (see below).

SPICING HOT OIL (*TARKA*, *BHAGAR*, *TEMPERADO*)

The technique of seasoning oil with whole and ground spices is very characteristic of Eastern cooking. The spicing of heated oil with curry leaves, turmeric, asafoetida, etc. before pouring on to cooked dishes such as lentils is a common way of finishing off a dish. The oil should always be heated over a low flame. The whole seeds should be allowed to sizzle, sputter or pop, as described above, with the lid of the pan left on. Again, care should be taken not to burn the oil as it would make the dish bitter.

ROASTING SPICES

Whole spices are best roasted over a low heat in a dry, heavy-based pan. Because of the varying sizes of individual spices, only one type at a time can be roasted. If the temperature is too high, the outside of the spice will be burned. You must remember that this process cannot be rushed, and if you burn the spices, the curries they are used in will taste bitter. Spices are roasted to give them a special flavour, and spices that have been lying around for a while can be given a new lease of life by roasting them.

FRYING WHOLE ALMONDS

First blanch the almonds by putting them into a pan of boiling water for 1 minute. Remove from the heat, drain, plunge the almonds into cold water and peel off the outer skins. Pat dry with kitchen paper. Heat oil to a depth of approximately 2.5cm/1in in a frying pan over a low to medium heat. Deep-fry for about 3–4 minutes until golden-brown. Drain on kitchen paper and leave until cold, then store for up to a week in an airtight jar.

Note: Whole cashews can be fried in the same way.

EXTRACTING THE ESSENCE FROM SAFFRON

Saffron is the most expensive spice available. It can be obtained in either powdered form or in strands. Spanish saffron is best. Whether you use the powder or the strands, saffron has to be dissolved in hot water before use. I usually grind the strands with a mortar and pestle and then dissolve the powder in a small quantity of hot water.

BASIC RECIPES

GARAM MASALA

For many Indian curries the basic spice mix known as garam masala is augmented with individual spices in proportions as required. Although ready-mixed packets of garam masala are widely available, it is better to grind fresh spices to produce your own mix, in a coffee grinder kept for this purpose. Here I give spice blends for three distinct types of garam masala.

GARAM MASALA I

(Sri Lankan curry powder)
1½ teaspoons coriander seeds
2 teaspoons cumin seeds
1 teaspoon fennel seeds
¼ teaspoon black peppercorns
5cm/2in cinnamon stick
6 cloves
5 cardamom pods
¼ teaspoon fenugreek seeds

GARAM MASALA II

1 tablespoon coriander seeds
1 tablespoon cumin seeds
½ teaspoon fenugreek seeds
1 teaspoon mustard seeds
¼ teaspoon asafoetida

GARAM MASALA III

2 tablespoons coriander seeds
1 tablespoon cumin seeds
1 teaspoon black peppercorns
1 teaspoon cardamom seeds
5cm/2in cinnamon stick
1 teaspoon cloves
½ nutmeg, freshly grated

1. Grind the spices of your choice to a fine powder in a coffee grinder (see page **20**).
2. Store in airtight jars in a cool, dark, dry place.

NOTE: Garam Masala (I) is used for Sri Lankan Chicken Curry (see page **142**). Garam Masala II is best suited for vegetable dishes, whilst Garam Masala III can be used in both meat and vegetable dishes.

GHEE

Ghee or clarified butter is an important ingredient in Indian cooking, in the preparation of both savoury dishes and desserts. It is also used for deep-frying. In making ghee, impurities are taken out from the butter fat, leaving a clear liquid which can be heated to a high temperature without burning.

225g/8oz unsalted butter

1. Melt the butter in a heavy-based saucepan over a very low heat. Allow to simmer for 10 minutes. Remove from the heat and, using a metal spoon, carefully skim away the white froth from the surface.
2. Return to the heat and simmer for a further 5 minutes. Turn off the heat and allow to cool for 10 minutes.
3. Using a very fine sieve, strain the melted fat. You should have a clear liquid which will solidify when completely cold. Pour into a jar with a tight-fitting lid and store in the refrigerator for up to 2 weeks.

CHICKEN STOCK

It takes very little effort to make stock at home, and there is no comparison between stock cubes and good home-made stock. (If you have to use stock cubes, remember that they contain salt, and adjust the salt in the recipe accordingly.)

To make a good stock, very slow simmering over a long period is necessary. Usually the stock is flavoured with onions, bay leaves and peppercorns.

1 chicken carcass
2 onions, chopped
10–12 black peppercorns
3 bay leaves
1.5 litres/2½ pints water

1. Put all the ingredients into a large saucepan and bring to the boil. Lower the heat to a simmer and cook, covered, for 2 hours.
2. Strain the stock and allow to cool, then refrigerate. Remove the surface layer of fat before use.

NOTE: Stock can be kept in the refrigerator for up to a week and also freezes well.

MEAT STOCK

500g/1¼lb lamb bones
2 onions, chopped
10–12 peppercorns
3 bay leaves
1.5 litres/2½ pints water

Prepare and store the stock as for chicken stock above.

RICE DISHES AND BREADS

RICE

BOILED RICE

Rice is a staple of the diet throughout much of Sri Lanka, India and Asia. Many varieties of rice are available in Britain. My particular favourite is basmati – a fragrant, long-grain rice with a distinctive aroma and flavour. The method of cooking rice described in this recipe (the absorption method) is the most popular in Asia. It is important to use the same cup for measuring both the rice and the water.

SERVES 2–3

1 cup basmati rice
1¾ cups cold water

1. Put the rice into a sieve and wash it under cold running water until the water runs clear. Since the rice absorbs water if left to soak, the washing should be done very quickly.
2. Put the rice into a saucepan and add the water. Bring rapidly to the boil. Stir, cover the pan, and cook for 15 minutes over a very low heat.
3. Remove the pan from the heat and allow the rice to stand for 10 minutes before serving. It is vital that the lid should be kept on during both cooking and standing. Fluff up the rice with a fork before serving, taking care not to damage the rice grains.

CURD RICE

(RICE WITH YOGURT)

The acid in the yogurt acts as a preservative. In South India tamarind or lemon juice is used instead of yogurt. This dish is often made to be eaten on journeys.

SERVES 2–3

1 tablespoon urad dhal
2 tablespoons chana dhal
1 cup boiling water
225g/8oz basmati rice
500ml/18fl oz cold water
2 tablespoons oil
½ teaspoon mustard seeds
10 curry leaves
4 dried red chillies
¼ teaspoon ground turmeric
a pinch of asafoetida
salt
500ml/18fl oz plain yogurt

1. Wash the urad and chana dhals together in a sieve, then soak them in the boiling water.
2. Wash the rice in a sieve under cold running water until the water runs clear. Since rice absorbs water if left to soak, the washing should be done very quickly.
3. Put the rice and water into a saucepan and bring rapidly to the boil. Give the rice a stir, cover the pan and cook for 15 minutes. Remove from the heat and allow to stand for 10 minutes before removing the lid.
4. Meanwhile, drain the dhals in a sieve.
5. Heat the oil in a small saucepan. Add the mustard seeds, cover and allow the seeds to pop over a low heat. Add the curry leaves, the chillies and chana and urad dhals.
6. Fry for a couple of minutes, over a low heat, stirring occasionally. Add the turmeric, asafoetida and salt to taste.
7. Put the yogurt into a large bowl. Pour the fried dhals mixture into the yogurt and mix thoroughly.
8. Fluff up the rice with a fork and mix into the spicy yogurt mixture. Serve cold.

KIRIBATH

(MILK RICE)

This is perhaps the most traditional of Sri Lankan rice dishes. It is usually made with unpolished rice that is red in colour. This dish is prepared for the Sinhalese New Year (in April) and for special occasions, and is served with a hot onion relish (see Lunumiris, page **167**), pieces of jaggery and bananas. I like to eat it with Ambul Thiyal (see page **121**) and Seeni Sambal (see page **166**).

SERVES 4

400g/14oz basmati rice
950ml/33fl oz cold water
100g/3½oz creamed coconut
400ml/14fl oz boiling water
salt

1. Wash the rice under cold running water until the water runs clear. Put the rice and water into a heavy-based saucepan and bring to the boil. Give the rice a stir, cover the pan, lower the heat to a simmer and cook for 15 minutes.
2. Meanwhile, dissolve the creamed coconut in the boiling water. Add salt to the creamed coconut.
3. Once the rice is cooked, the next stage requires your constant attention. Pour the coconut liquid into the rice and stir over a low heat until the rice has absorbed the liquid. In Sri Lanka this is done with the handle of a wooden spoon in order to minimize damage to the grains of rice.
4. Once the liquid has been absorbed, spread the rice out on a flat dish or platter. Using a spatula, flatten and smooth out the top. Cut into diamond shapes about 7.5cm/3in long. When the rice cools it holds its shape and you should be able to serve pieces of *kiribath* on individual plates.

KAHABATH

(COCONUT MILK RICE)

Literally meaning 'yellow rice', this Sri Lankan speciality is cooked in coconut milk. It is often made on special occasions and is always served with Sri Lankan Chicken Curry, fried aubergines and potato curry (see pages **142, 143, 61** and **72**).

SERVES 4

310g/11oz basmati rice
2 tablespoons oil or ghee (see page **32***)*
½ medium onion, finely chopped
10 curry leaves
1 stalk lemon grass (optional)
5cm/2in screwpine (optional)
8 black peppercorns
4 cloves
5 cardamom pods
5cm/2in stick cinnamon
750ml/1⅓ pints boiling water
¼ teaspoon ground turmeric
salt
55g/2oz creamed coconut, finely chopped

To garnish
deep-fried onions (see page **27***)*
fried whole cashew nuts (see page **28***)*

1. Wash the rice in a sieve under cold running water until the water runs clear. Since rice absorbs water if left to soak, the washing should be done very quickly. Allow to drain thoroughly.
2. Heat the oil or ghee in a heavy-based saucepan. Add the onion, curry leaves, lemon grass and screwpine, if using, and the peppercorns, cloves, cardamoms and cinnamon. Fry over a low to medium heat until the onion is golden-brown.
3. Add the rice (which should be quite dry) and fry for 1 minute. Now add the boiling water, turmeric, salt to taste and the creamed coconut. Bring to the boil and stir to make sure the coconut is dissolved. (Alternatively the coconut can be dissolved in the boiling water prior to adding to the rice.) Cover the pan, lower the heat and simmer for 15 minutes.
4. Remove from the heat and allow to stand for 10 minutes. Garnish with deep-fried onions (see page **27**) and fried cashew nuts (see page **28**) and serve hot.

BATH TEMPERADU

(SRI LANKAN FRIED RICE)

In Sri Lanka fried rice is made from samba rice, which is a pearly-white grain. Usually only vegetables are added to the already cooked rice. However, there is a modern tendency to mix in prawns, bacon and meat, and to flavour the rice with soy sauce.

SERVES 6

2 cups basmati rice
3¼ cups cold water
55g/2oz ghee (see page **32**) *or oil*
1 medium onion, finely chopped
15 curry leaves
5cm/2in screwpine
2 carrots, grated
2 leeks, finely shredded
55g/2oz white cabbage, finely shredded
1 green pepper, deseeded and finely chopped
55g/2oz frozen peas, defrosted
salt

1. Put the rice into a sieve and wash under cold running water until the water runs clear. Since rice absorbs water if left to soak, the washing should be done very quickly.
2. Put the rice into a saucepan and add the water. Bring rapidly to the boil. Give the rice a stir, cover the pan and cook over a very low heat for 15 minutes.
3. Remove the pan from the heat and leave the rice to get cold.
4. Heat the ghee in a large saucepan. Add the onion, curry leaves and screwpine and fry until the onion is lightly browned. Add the carrots, leeks, cabbage, pepper, peas and salt to taste. Stir until well mixed. Cover the pan and cook for 2 minutes over a low heat.
5. Fluff up the rice with a fork and add gradually to the vegetables, stirring after each addition to ensure that the dish is well mixed. Remove from the heat and pile on to a serving platter. Serve hot.

YAKHNI PULAO

(STOCK RICE)

This is a special rice dish in which the rice is cooked in chicken stock. Use home-made stock for best results.

SERVES 2–3

225g/8oz basmati rice
2 tablespoons ghee (see page **32***) or vegetable oil*
6 cardamom pods
5cm/2in cinnamon stick
6 cloves
5 black peppercorns
4 bay leaves
500ml/18fl oz chicken stock (see page **33***)*
salt

To garnish
1 onion, sliced and deep-fried (see page **27***)*

1. Put the rice into a sieve and wash under cold running water until the water runs clear. Since rice absorbs water if left to soak, the washing should be done very quickly. Allow to drain thoroughly.
2. Heat the ghee or oil in a heavy-based saucepan over a medium heat. Add the cardamom, cinnamon, cloves, peppercorns and bay leaves and fry for 1 minute. Add the drained rice and fry over a low heat for 1 minute, stirring constantly.
3. In a separate saucepan, heat the stock to near-boiling point. Add the hot stock to the rice with the rice mixture and salt to taste and bring rapidly to the boil. Cover the pan and cook over a low heat for 15 minutes. Allow the rice to stand for 10 minutes before removing the lid.
4. Serve garnished with deep-fried onion.

KICHIRI

(LENTIL RICE)

This is a traditional vegetarian dish which combines lentils and rice. It is often served with a warm, spicy yogurt sauce – *khadi* – pickles and pappadams. In South India orange lentils are used instead of the yellow mung ones. Serve with Saar (see page **111**).

SERVES 4

200g/7oz yellow mung lentils
200g/7oz basmati rice
2 tablespoons vegetable oil
1 small onion, chopped
6 curry leaves
½ teaspoon ground cumin
½ teaspoon ground coriander
¼ teaspoon ground turmeric
salt
1 litre/1¾ pints boiling water

1. Pick over the lentils, wash them in several changes of cold water and leave to soak in cold water for 30 minutes, then put into a sieve and leave to drain.
2. Put the rice into a sieve and wash under cold running water until the water runs clear. Since rice absorbs water if left to soak, the washing should be done very quickly. Leave the rice to drain.
3. Heat the oil in a medium heavy-based saucepan and fry the onion and curry leaves until the onion is barely brown. Add the spices and fry for 30 seconds.
4. Add the drained lentils and rice to the pan and stir until well mixed. Add salt to taste and the boiling water and bring back to the boil. Give the mixture a stir, lower the heat to a simmer and cook, covered, for 20 minutes.
5. Remove from the heat and allow to stand for 10 minutes before serving.

NOTE: This lentil/rice dish is fairly moist compared with, say, plain boiled rice.

SABZI PULAO

(VEGETABLE RICE)

This rice-cum-vegetable dish could be the focal point of a vegetarian meal or it could be eaten with any meat or fish curry.

SERVES 2–3

225g/8oz basmati rice
4 tablespoons oil
½ teaspoon cumin seeds
1 medium onion, finely chopped
1 small potato, finely diced
110g/4oz frozen peas.
500ml/18fl oz boiling water
salt

1. Wash the rice in a sieve under cold running water until the water runs clear. Since rice absorbs water if left to soak, the washing should be done very quickly. Allow to drain thoroughly.
2. Heat the oil in a saucepan, add the cumin seeds, cover and sizzle for 4 seconds over a low heat or until lightly browned. (Care should be taken not to overheat the oil or the cumin seeds will burn.) Add the onion and potato and cook until lightly browned. Add the drained rice and fry for a few seconds.
3. Add the peas, water and salt to taste, and bring to the boil. Give the mixture a stir, cover the pan and simmer for 15 minutes. Remove from the heat and allow to stand for 10 minutes before serving.

VEGETABLE PULAO

This rice dish is delicately flavoured with saffron and vegetables. It can be served with meat, fish, lentils or vegetable curries.

SERVES 4

2 cups basmati rice
2 tablespoons ghee (see page **32***)*
1 onion, finely chopped
6 cloves
6 cardamom pods
5cm/2in cinnamon stick
3 curry leaves
1 red pepper, deseeded and chopped
1 green pepper, deseeded and chopped
2 leeks, thinly sliced
2 carrots, grated
3 cups boiling water
1 sachet/½ teaspoon saffron powder, dissolved in 2 teaspoons hot water
salt

To garnish
deep-fried onions (see page **27***)*
deep-fried whole almonds (see page **28***)*

1. Wash the rice in a sieve under cold running water until the water runs clear. Since rice absorbs water if left to soak, the washing should be done very quickly. Allow to drain thoroughly.
2. Heat the ghee in a medium saucepan. Add the onion, cloves, cardamom, cinnamon and curry leaves. Fry until the onions are lightly browned.
3. Add the rice and fry for about 2 minutes over a low heat. Add all the vegetables and mix thoroughly. Add the boiling water, saffron liquid and salt to taste and bring rapidly to the boil. Give the mixture a stir, cover and simmer for 15 minutes over the lowest possible heat.
4. Remove from the heat and allow the mixture to stand for 10 minutes before removing the lid. Fluff up the rice with a fork. Garnish with deep-fried onions and fried whole almonds.

LAMB BIRIANI

An exotic combination of meat, rice and spices that is perhaps the most famous of Moghul dishes. It is eaten throughout the Muslim world on festive occasions. I have eaten a Kurdish version where the biriani was encased in pastry for the final cooking.

SERVES 4

800g/1¾lb leg of lamb
1 teaspoon ground cumin
1 teaspoon ground coriander
½ teaspoon freshly grated nutmeg
8 cloves
10 cardamom pods
5cm/2in cinnamon stick
8 black peppercorns
290ml/½ pint plain low-fat yogurt
5 cloves of garlic
5cm/2in piece of fresh root ginger, peeled
55g/2oz coriander leaves
1 large onion, roughly chopped
salt
2 tablespoons oil
½ medium onion, thinly sliced

For the stock
1 onion, chopped
2 bay leaves
10 black peppercorns
1.5 litres/2½ pints water

For the rice
*2–3 tablespoons ghee (see page **32**)*
2 bay leaves
5cm/2in cinnamon stick
5 cloves
6 cardamom pods
400g/14oz basmati rice, washed and drained
1 teaspoon saffron powder, dissolved in 1 teaspoon hot water
salt

For the garnish
oil for deep-frying
55g/2oz blanched whole almonds
55g/2oz sultanas
30g/1oz dried onion flakes

1. Trim away any fat from the leg of lamb and cut the meat into 1cm/½in cubes. To make the stock: put the lamb bone into a large saucepan, add the onion, bay leaves, peppercorns and water and bring to the boil. Lower the heat and simmer until it is reduced by half. Strain the stock and reserve.
2. Put the cumin, coriander, nutmeg, cloves, cardamoms, cinnamon and peppercorns into an electric grinder and grind to a fine powder (see page **20**).
3. In a liquidizer or food processor, blend the yogurt, garlic, ginger, coriander leaves and chopped onion to a paste. In a large bowl, combine the ground ingredients with the blended ingredients. Put in the cubes of meat and stir until well coated in the marinade. Leave to marinate for 6 hours.
4. Heat the oil in a heavy-based saucepan and fry the onion until golden-brown. Then add the marinated lamb and cook over a medium heat for

10 minutes, stirring. Add the remaining marinade and bring to the boil. Cover and simmer until the liquid has evaporated.

5. To prepare the rice: bring the stock to the boil. Heat the ghee in a large, heavy-based saucepan. Add the bay leaves, cinnamon, cloves, cardamoms and rice, and fry over a low heat for 2 minutes. Add the meat, 800ml/1⅓ pints of the stock, saffron liquid and salt to taste and bring rapidly to the boil. Lower the heat, cover the pan and simmer for 15 minutes. Remove from the heat and allow to stand for 10 minutes before serving.

6. To prepare the garnish: heat the oil in a small pan, over a low to medium heat. Fry the almonds until golden-brown. Drain and reserve. Add the sultanas and remove them as soon as they plump up. Lastly, add the onion flakes and remove from the oil almost immediately as they hardly take a second to brown.

7. Pile the biriani on to a large serving dish or platter and garnish with the almonds, sultanas and onion flakes. Serve hot.

CHICKEN BIRIANI

Perhaps the most popular rice dish throughout the Muslim world. This dish combines chicken and rice and there are several versions of it. Traditionally, the final cooking is done by steaming the layered rice and meat in a sealed container. This dish is often made for special festivals and feasts.

SERVES 4

For the chicken
½ teaspoon ground cumin
½ teaspoon ground coriander
½ teaspoon paprika
¼ teaspoon ground turmeric
¼ teaspoon ground cloves
½ teaspoon ground cardamom
1 teaspoon ground cinnamon
1 green chilli (optional)
1 medium onion
5 cloves of garlic
30g/1oz coriander leaves
1 tablespoon peeled and finely chopped fresh root ginger
½ tablespoon tomato purée
salt
225ml/8fl oz plain yogurt
450g/1lb boneless chicken

For the rice
2 tablespoons ghee (see page **32***), butter or oil*
½ medium onion, finely chopped
400g/14oz basmati rice, washed and drained
500ml/18fl oz chicken stock
salt
½ teaspoon saffron powder, dissolved in 2 teaspoons hot water

To garnish
55g/2oz deep-fried cashew nuts (see page **28***)*
225g/8oz deep-fried onions

1. To prepare the chicken: blend all the ingredients, except the chicken, in a liquidizer, until smooth. Cut the chicken into bite-sized pieces. Marinate the chicken in the spicy yogurt mixture for at least 4 hours.
2. To prepare the rice: grease a large casserole dish.
3. Heat half the ghee, butter or oil in a saucepan and fry the onion until golden-brown. Add the rice and fry over a low heat for 5 minutes, until the grains become translucent. Add the stock and bring to the boil. Cover the pan and simmer for 10 minutes.
4. While the rice is cooking, heat the remaining ghee, butter or oil in a frying pan and quickly fry the chicken pieces for a minute. Pour in the marinade and simmer for 5 minutes. Preheat the oven to 160°C/325°F/gas mark 3.
5. Place one-third of the rice at the bottom of the casserole dish. Put half the chicken over the rice and cover with half the remaining rice. Put in the remaining chicken and cover with the remaining rice.
6. Measure the marinade liquid and add hot water if necessary to make it up to 225ml/8fl oz. Add the saffron liquid to

the marinade and pour over the casserole. Cover and bake in the preheated oven for 45 minutes.
7. Garnish with the deep-fried cashew nuts and onions just before serving.

BREADS

CHAPATIS

Chapati is the most basic form of unleavened bread and is eaten throughout India. It is sold by street vendors who cook the chapatis on makeshift hearths and sell them to passersby. It is traditionally cooked on a concave iron plate (*tava*) which is heated to a high temperature. The flour used in the preparation of chapatis is called *ata* and is available at most Indian shops. However, equally delicious results can be obtained by combining wholemeal flour with plain flour. The success of a chapati is in its cooking. It has to be cooked quickly over high heat to prevent it from becoming hard and leathery. It is usually smeared with ghee after cooking and is eaten with vegetables at the beginning of a meal.

SERVES 4

100g/3½oz plain flour
100g/3½oz superfine wholemeal flour
salt
about 150ml/¼ pint tepid water
100g/3½oz ghee (see page **32***) or unsalted butter*

1. In a bowl, combine the flours and salt to taste. Add sufficient water to mix to a soft, pliable dough. Knead the dough for 5 minutes, then cover and allow to rest at room temperature for 10 minutes.
2. Divide the dough into 8 equal portions. Now put the griddle to heat over a medium flame. On a floured surface roll out each portion of dough to form a 15cm/6in disc. Keep the rolled chapatis covered with a damp cloth to prevent drying while you cook them one at a time. Remove the excess surface flour before cooking by holding the chapati in the palms of your hands and gently slapping it.
3. Place the chapati on the hot griddle for 7–10 seconds, then turn it over. Allow the chapati to brown on the other side. Depending on the heat of the griddle this should take about 15 seconds. Turn the chapati over again and using a folded tea-towel, apply gentle pressure to it in several places to encourage it to balloon up. It is this puffing-up process that gives the chapati its light texture. In India this is done by placing the chapati on a naked flame. Smear the hot chapati with a knob of ghee or butter, and leave covered with a tea-towel until all the chapatis are cooked.

POORI

(DEEP-FRIED UNLEAVENED BREAD)

Pooris are usually eaten at the start of a meal with vegetables. Children often take pooris to school in their lunch-boxes.

SERVES 4

100g/3½oz superfine wholemeal flour
100g/3½oz plain flour
salt
2 teaspoons oil
150–170ml/5–6fl oz tepid water
oil for deep-frying

1. In a bowl combine the flours, salt to taste, the oil and sufficient water to mix to a soft, pliable dough. Knead the dough for 1 minute until smooth. Cover and leave at room temperature for 20 minutes. Pooris are usually rolled out one at a time but I find it easier to roll out the dough to a thickness of approximately 3mm/⅙in and then to cut 7.5–10cm/3–4in discs of dough with a pastry cutter. Leave the discs covered with a damp cloth while you fry them one at a time.
2. Heat the oil until almost smoking hot. Put in a poori and when it begins to rise to the surface, gently pat it down with the back of a spoon to keep it submerged in the oil. This gentle pressure encourages the poori to puff up like a balloon. Once this happens, turn the poori over and cook for a couple of seconds on the other side. Drain on a cooling rack. Repeat the frying process until the dough is used up.

METHI POORI

(DEEP-FRIED UNLEAVENED BREAD WITH FENUGREEK LEAVES)

By combining gram flour with wholemeal and plain white flour, these pooris stay crisp for longer. Since fenugreek leaves can only be bought at specialist stores, you can substitute coriander leaves. I first tasted these pooris when my friend Mangala made them to be eaten on the train from Poona to Hyderabad.

SERVES 4

100g/3½oz plain flour
100g/3½oz superfine wholemeal flour
100g/3½oz gram flour
salt
5 tablespoons chopped fenugreek leaves
2 tablespoons oil
about 175ml/6fl oz tepid water
oil for deep-frying

1. In a bowl, combine the flours with salt to taste and the fenugreek leaves. Dribble in the oil and sufficient water to mix to a pliable dough. Knead the dough for 2 minutes, then cover and leave at room temperature for 10 minutes.
2. Roll out the dough to a 3mm/⅙in thickness. Using a pastry cutter, cut into 7.5cm/3in discs. Leave the discs covered with a damp cloth to prevent drying while you fry the pooris one at a time.
3. Heat the oil over a medium heat until hot. Test the temperature by putting in a small piece of the dough. If the dough rises to the surface in a couple of seconds the oil is ready for frying the pooris. Put a poori into the hot oil and when it rises to the surface, gently push it down, using the back of a spoon, to keep it submerged in the hot oil until it puffs up. Turn over and cook until the other side is lightly browned. Drain on a cooling rack.

The frying process should take about 15–20 seconds for each poori. Continue until all the dough is used up and about 30 pooris made. Once cold, store in an airtight tin for up to a day.

NAAN

(LEAVENED BREAD)

Naan is the most popular Indian leavened bread. It is traditionally cooked in a clay oven (*tandoor*). The naans, which are traditionally tear-shaped, are slapped on to the walls of the *tandoor*. The intensity of heat in a *tandoor* is not easy to achieve in a domestic oven, but by cooking the naans in a very hot oven for a short time a reasonable result can be obtained.

SERVES 4

500g/18oz strong white flour
1 sachet easy-blend dried yeast
2 teaspoons kalonji (black onion seeds)
salt
½ teaspoon baking powder
1 egg, beaten
2 tablespoons oil
200ml/7fl oz Greek yogurt
150ml/¼ pint tepid semi-skimmed milk
oil for brushing

1. Sieve the flour into a large bowl. Add the yeast, kalonji, salt to taste and the baking powder. In another bowl mix together the egg, oil, yogurt and 140ml/4fl oz of the milk. Pour into the flour and mix to a soft dough. If the dough seems dry add the remaining milk. Knead for 5 minutes until smooth and elastic. Cover and leave in a warm place until doubled in size.

2. Preheat the oven to 220°C/425°F/gas mark 7. Place a roasting tin half-filled with water at the bottom of the oven. This provides moisture which prevents the naans from drying out too quickly.

3. Punch down the dough and divide into 10 equal portions. Using the tips of your fingers, spread out a portion of dough on a greased baking tray to the size of a pitta bread. Brush the surface with oil.

4. Bake on the top shelf of the preheated oven for 7 minutes. Turn the naans over and bake for a further 5 minutes. Remove from the oven and cover with a cloth to keep the naans warm. Repeat until all the dough has been used. While the naans are baking, the uncooked dough should be kept covered. Refill the baking tray with boiling water when necessary.

ROTI

(COCONUT BREAD)

This is a Sri Lankan breakfast speciality which is usually eaten with a hot onion chutney – Lunumiris (see page **165**). It is usually made with roasted rice flour but plain-flour rotis taste equally delicious. As children we used to eat them smeared with butter and jam.

SERVES 3

225g/8oz plain flour
85g/3oz desiccated coconut
salt
150–170ml/5–6fl oz tepid water

1. In a bowl, combine the flour, coconut and salt to taste. Make a well in the centre and add sufficient water to mix to a stiff dough. If the dough seems too stiff to handle, add a little more water. Knead thoroughly. Mix the dough into 6 equal portions.
2. On a greased surface, using your fingertips, flatten out each portion to resemble an average-sized plate. (In Sri Lanka rotis are flattened out on banana leaves.)
3. Heat a griddle or a heavy-based frying pan over a low heat. Place a roti in the pan and cook until brown flecks appear on the bottom side. Turn over and brown the other side. Repeat until all the rotis are cooked.

PARATHAS

(FRIED UNLEAVENED BREAD)

Parathas are yet another form of unleavened bread, and, like chapatis, need quick cooking to ensure that they remain soft.

SERVES 3–4

200g/7oz superfine wholemeal flour
200g/7oz plain flour
salt
2 tablespoons oil
about 290–300ml/9–10fl oz water
oil for cooking and brushing

1. In a large bowl combine the flours and the salt to taste. Dribble in the oil. Add enough water to mix to a pliable dough. Knead until smooth.
2. Divide the dough into 12 equal portions. Roll each portion to a 15cm/6in disc. Using a pastry brush, cover the surface of each paratha with a very thin coating of oil. Fold in half and brush the semi-circle again thinly with oil. Fold again to form a quadrant (quarter-circle). Roll out each quadrant to roughly three times its original dimension. The parathas, which are now ready to cook, should be roughly triangular in shape. (When rolling out the parathas do not dust with a lot of flour as the surface flour will burn during cooking.) Cover the rolled-out parathas with a damp cloth while you cook them one at a time.
3. Heat a griddle or a heavy-based frying pan over a medium heat. Put in enough oil to lightly coat the surface of the griddle or pan. Put a paratha on to the griddle or pan and cook for 1 minute. Turn over and cook for 1 further minute or until the surface has brown flecks. Repeat the process until all the parathas are cooked.

STUFFED PARATHAS

(STUFFED FRIED UNLEAVENED BREAD)

This slightly more elaborate version of parathas (see previous recipe) is eaten on special occasions.

SERVES 4

200g/7oz superfine wholemeal flour
200g/7oz plain flour
salt
1 tablespoon ghee (see page **32***)*
290ml/9fl oz tepid water
225g/8oz potatoes
2 tablespoons oil
¼ teaspoon mustard seeds
½ medium onion, finely chopped
⅛ teaspoon turmeric
⅛ teaspoon asafoetida
ghee or oil for shallow-frying and brushing

1. In a bowl, combine the flours and salt to taste. Rub in the tablespoon of ghee. Make a well in the centre of the flour and gradually add sufficient water to mix to a soft, pliable dough. Care should be taken to add the water a little at a time, as it is very difficult to prescribe an exact quantity for the particular type of flour you may be using. Knead the dough for about 5 minutes, and then cover and leave at room temperature for 1 hour.
2. Wash the potatoes, put them into a saucepan of water and bring to the boil. Lower the heat and simmer until cooked. Remove the skins and mash the potatoes.
3. Heat the 2 tablespoons of oil in a saucepan. Put in the mustard seeds, cover and allow to sputter over a low heat. Add the onion and fry gently for 1 minute. Add the turmeric, asafoetida and ½ teaspoon salt. Stir until well mixed. Mix in the mashed potatoes and cook over a low heat until the mixture leaves the sides of the pan. Remove from the heat and allow to cool.
4. Divide the dough into 10 equal portions. Roll out each portion of dough to resemble a fine pancake. Take a teaspoonful of the potato filling and spread it evenly over half the rolled-out disc of dough and fold to form a semi-circle. Brush oil on half the surface and fold over once more to form a quadrant (quarter-circle). Roll out the quadrant until twice the size.
5. Heat a tablespoon of oil or ghee in a heavy-based frying pan or *tava*. Fry each quadrant for about 2–3 minutes on each side until brown flecks appear on the paratha. Repeat until all the parathas are cooked. Serve warm.

NOTE: Parathas can be reheated either in a microwave oven, or wrapped in foil in a conventional oven preheated to 180°C/350°F/gas mark 4 for 10 minutes.

INDIAPPAM

(SAVOURY RICE STICKS)

This Sri Lankan and Kerala speciality of rice vermicelli is made from roasted rice flour which is made into a stiff dough and pressed through a perforated disc on to special woven mats. The mats are stacked one on top of the other and steamed. Ready-to-use rice sticks are available in Indian and Chinese shops.

SERVES 4

225/8oz rice sticks
3 tablespoons oil
½ medium onion, chopped
10 curry leaves
2 carrots, grated
2 leeks, finely shredded
1 green pepper, deseeded and chopped
2 tablespoons tomato ketchup
1 tablespoon soy sauce
1 teaspoon salt

To garnish
110g/4oz cooked peas
55g/2oz deep-fried cashew nuts (see page **28***)*
2 tablespoons deep-fried chopped onions (see page **27***)*
3 hard-boiled eggs, cut into wedges
55g/2oz sautéed mushrooms

1. Soak the rice sticks in very cold water for 30 minutes.
2. Bring a large saucepan to the boil. Drain the rice sticks in a colander and put into the boiling water. Remove from the heat and leave in the hot water for 3 minutes. Drain and put back into very cold water before you proceed to the next stage.
3. Heat the oil in a large frying pan and fry the onion and curry leaves until the onion is lightly browned. Add the carrots, leeks and pepper and stir-fry for 1 minute. Add the ketchup, soy sauce and salt. Drain the rice sticks and add to the pan, and mix thoroughly over a low heat, stirring constantly to prevent the rice sticks from sticking.
4. Transfer to a large serving platter and garnish attractively with the peas, cashew nuts, onions, hard-boiled eggs and mushrooms.

NOTE: This dish is usually served with chicken or prawn curry (see pages **142–44** and **124**).

VEGETABLES

FRIED AUBERGINE DISCS

These are very easy to make and can form part of any spicy meal.

SERVES 4

225g/8oz aubergine
salt
55g/2oz gram flour
¼ teaspoon chilli powder (optional)
oil for frying

1. Wash the aubergine and trim off the stalk. Cut the aubergine crosswise into 1cm/½in thick slices.
2. Sprinkle the aubergine slices with salt and leave for 30 minutes. Rinse quickly under cold running water and pat dry with kitchen paper.
3. Sieve the gram flour on to a large plate. Add the chilli powder, if using, and salt to taste.
4. Heat 1cm/½in oil in a large frying pan or skillet over a medium heat. While the oil is heating, dip the aubergine discs in the seasoned flour, then add to the hot oil. Fry for about 30 seconds, then turn the discs over and fry for a further 30 seconds or until the discs have a golden-brown crust on both sides. Drain on a cooling rack for 1 minute, then serve immediately.

VAMBOTU PAHI

(AUBERGINE CURRY)

This aubergine preparation is made on special occasions. It is often served with Kahabath (see page **40**) and Sri Lankan Chicken Curry (see pages **142 and 143**).

SERVES 4

600g/1¼lb aubergines
salt
oil for deep-frying
2 tablespoons oil
½ medium onion, finely chopped
¼ teaspoon ground turmeric
1 teaspoon ground cumin
1 teaspoon ground coriander
1 teaspoon ground black mustard seeds
4 cloves of garlic, finely chopped
2.5cm/1in piece of fresh root ginger, peeled and grated
3 green chillies, chopped
10 curry leaves
1 tablespoon malt vinegar
4 tablespoons water
2 tablespoons coconut milk powder
½ teaspoon sugar

1. Wash the aubergines and remove the stalks. Cut each aubergine lengthwise into 4 slices. Sprinkle with salt and leave in a single layer, uncovered, for 30 minutes.
2. Rinse the aubergines quickly under cold running water and pat dry with kitchen paper. Cut each slice lengthwise into strips, then into 2.5cm/1in cubes.
3. Deep-fry the aubergine cubes a few at a time in hot oil until golden-brown. Drain thoroughly on kitchen paper.
4. Heat the 2 tablespoons oil in a medium saucepan and fry the onion until golden-brown. Add the turmeric, cumin, coriander and mustard and stir for a couple of seconds. Add the garlic, ginger, chillies and curry leaves. Remove the pan from the heat and drain off excess oil. Add the vinegar, water, coconut milk powder, salt to taste and the sugar and bring slowly to the boil. Add the fried aubergine cubes, stir and simmer over a low heat until most of the liquid has evaporated.

BAIGAN BHARTA

(ROASTED AUBERGINES)

The aubergines taste best when roasted on a coal fire. However, although oven-roasting doesn't impart a smoky flavour, the aubergines taste good too when cooked in this way.

SERVES 2

400g/14oz aubergines
2 tablespoons oil
1 teaspoon cumin seeds
½ medium onion, finely chopped
¼ teaspoon ground turmeric
2 green chillies, chopped
2 ripe tomatoes, chopped
salt

To garnish
coriander leaves

1. Preheat the oven to 200°C/400°F/gas mark 6. Wash the aubergines and pat dry with kitchen paper. Put the aubergines on a baking tray and roast in the middle of the preheated oven for 30–40 minutes or until a skewer goes through easily when inserted.
2. Remove the aubergines from the oven, cut off the stalk, peel away the skin and mash the pulp with a fork.
3. Heat the oil in a small saucepan. Add the cumin seeds, cover and allow to sizzle. Then add the onion and fry until softened. Add the turmeric, chillies and tomatoes and fry for 3 minutes. Add the aubergine pulp and stir over a low heat until well mixed. Just before serving, add salt to taste and garnish with coriander leaves.

BHINDI BHAJI

(CURRIED OKRA)

Okra is a very versatile vegetable eaten throughout the Indian sub-continent. It can be fried, steamed, boiled or stuffed. When choosing okra make sure that they are a shiny green colour and are flexible at the stalk end. Always wash and pat dry before using.

SERVES 4

450g/1lb okra
2 tablespoons oil
1 small onion, finely chopped
½ teaspoon ground cumin
½ teaspoon ground coriander
½ teaspoon chilli powder (optional)
¼ teaspoon ground turmeric
salt
150g/5oz canned tomatoes

1. Wash the okra and pat dry with kitchen paper. Trim off the tops and tails and cut the okra into 2.5cm/1in pieces.
2. Heat the oil in a wide-bottomed pan over a low to medium heat and fry the onion until lightly browned. Add the spices, salt to taste and the tomatoes and fry for 1 minute until well mixed. Add the okra and stir until well coated in the spicy tomato mixture. Bring to the boil. Cover and simmer for 5 minutes or until the okra is cooked and all the liquid absorbed. The finished dish should not have any liquid.

BANDAKKA BADUM

(CURRIED FRIED OKRA)

Deep-frying vegetables before currying them is a method used for special occasions.

SERVES 4

450g/1lb okra
oil for deep-frying
1 tablespoon oil
1 small onion, finely chopped
½ teaspoon chilli powder (optional)
¼ teaspoon ground turmeric
½ teaspoon ground cumin
¼ teaspoon ground coriander
1 cup water
30g/1oz creamed coconut
salt

1. Wash the okra and pat dry with kitchen paper. Trim off the tops and cut the okra into 2.5cm/1in pieces.
2. Deep-fry the okra pieces in hot oil until golden-brown.
3. Heat the tablespoon of oil in a saucepan and fry the onion until lightly browned. Add the spices, water and creamed coconut, season to taste and bring to the boil.
4. Just prior to serving add the okra, bring rapidly to the boil and stir until well mixed. Serve with rice.

GOJU

(SPICY OKRA)

This Karnataka (a district in South India) recipe for okra can also be used for bitter gourd, see page **84**. When dry-roasting the spices (see page **28**), care should be taken not to burn them.

SERVES 2–3

For the masala
3 tablespoons desiccated coconut
1 tablespoon sesame seeds
1 tablespoon coriander seeds
1 tablespoon chana dhal
½ teaspoon black peppercorns

400g/14oz okra
3 tablespoons oil
½ teaspoon black mustard seeds
2 dried red chillies (optional)
10 curry leaves
¼ teaspoon ground turmeric
salt
425ml/¾ pint water

1. To make the masala: in a heavy-based frying pan, dry-roast the coconut and sesame seeds until the coconut is lightly browned. Then dry-roast the coriander and chana dhal until the coriander seeds are a little darker than they normally are. Grind the coconut, sesame, chana dhal, coriander and peppercorns to a fine powder in a coffee grinder (see page **20**).

2. Wash the okra and pat dry with kitchen paper. Trim off the tops and tails. Cut the okra into 1cm/½in pieces. Heat the oil in a medium saucepan. Add the mustard seeds, cover and allow to pop over a low heat. Add the chillies, if using, and the curry leaves, and fry for 30 seconds or until the curry leaves are lightly browned. Add the okra and the turmeric and fry for a few seconds until the okra is coated in the oil. Add the ground spices, salt to taste and the water and bring to the boil. Simmer for 15 minutes, or until the okra is cooked.

BHINDI THORAN

(OKRA WITH COCONUT)

This South Indian preparation from Kerala brings out the natural flavour of the okra; it is very slightly spiced and flavoured with coconut.

SERVES 2

225g/8oz okra
2 tablespoons vegetable oil
1 teaspoon mustard seeds
10 curry leaves
¼ teaspoon ground turmeric
2 green chillies, chopped
salt
2 tablespoons cold water

To garnish
2 teaspoons fresh or desiccated coconut

1. Wash the okra and pat dry with kitchen paper. Trim off the tops and tails and cut the okra into 2.5cm/1in pieces.
2. Heat the oil in a medium saucepan over a medium heat. Add the mustard seeds, cover and allow to sputter over a low heat. Add the curry leaves and fry for 30 seconds. Add the turmeric, chillies, salt to taste and the okra and stir until well mixed. Add the water, cover and cook until the okra is tender. The cooked dish should be green in colour. Overcooking will tend to make the okra brown. Garnish with coconut and serve.

STUFFED OKRA

This is a delicious North Indian speciality.

SERVES 4

450g/1lb okra
85g/3oz desiccated coconut
½ teaspoon ground cumin powder
¼ teaspoon ground chilli
¼ teaspoon ground turmeric
juice of ½ lemon
salt
75ml/3fl oz oil

1. Wash the okra and pat dry with kitchen paper.
2. Slit each okra lengthwise to make a pocket, taking care not to cut right through.
3. In a bowl, mix together all the ingredients except the okra and the oil. Place in a piping bag.
4. Carefully pipe a small quantity of the coconut filling into each pocket.
5. Heat the oil in a large frying pan. Carefully arrange the stuffed okra in a single layer in the pan and fry for 5 minutes. Turn the okra over and cook for a further 5 minutes, adding a little more oil if necessary.

SAAG BHAJI

(COOKED SPINACH)

Greens form an important part of the diet of the Indian sub-continent as they are relatively cheap. Many varieties of leafy vegetable are available and any greens can be substituted for the spinach in this recipe.

SERVES 4

450g/1lb spinach
2 tablespoons oil
¼ teaspoon black mustard seeds
¼ teaspoon cumin seeds
⅛ teaspoon ground turmeric
½ teaspoon ground coriander
½ teaspoon ground cumin
1 tomato, finely chopped
salt

1. Wash the spinach leaf by leaf under cold running water to get rid of any sand or grit.
2. Place in a colander or strainer to drain most of the water and roughly chop the spinach.
3. Heat the oil in a medium saucepan. Add the mustard and cumin seeds, cover and allow to pop over a low heat. Add the turmeric, coriander and cumin and stir for a couple of seconds. Add the tomato and salt to taste and mix thoroughly. Increase the heat and add the spinach, a handful at a time, stir-frying after each addition. The spinach will reduce greatly in volume and only requires about 3 minutes' cooking.

ALA SUDHATA

(WHITE POTATO CURRY)

In Sri Lanka curries are often described by their colour (white, red or black). This mild potato curry is referred to as a white curry although in reality it is pale yellow due to the turmeric in it. The fenugreek seeds need to be soaked for at least 3 hours before cooking.

SERVES 4

500g/18oz potatoes
½ teaspoon fenugreek seeds
¼ teaspoon ground turmeric
½ onion, finely chopped
5cm/2in cinnamon stick
2 green chillies, chopped
10 curry leaves
3 tablespoons coconut milk powder
salt

1. Wash and peel the potatoes, and cut into 2.5cm/1in cubes.
2. Put the potatoes, fenugreek, turmeric, onion, cinnamon, chillies and curry leaves into a medium saucepan. Cover generously with water and bring to the boil. Cover the pan and simmer for 10 minutes or until the potatoes are cooked. There should be about a cup of water left. Add the coconut milk powder and salt to taste and simmer, uncovered, for a further 3 minutes.

ALA THEL DHAALA

(SPICE-FRIED POTATOES)

These potatoes are hot and are usually eaten with fried rice or any special rice dish such as *kahabath* (see page **40**).

SERVES 4

450g/1lb potatoes
oil for deep-frying
225g/8oz onions, thinly sliced
1 tablespoon vegetable oil
1 tablespoon Maldive fish, powdered (optional)
a few curry leaves
½ teaspoon coarse chilli powder
salt
2 teaspoons lime or lemon juice

1. Wash the potatoes and place them in a saucepan. Cover with cold water and bring rapidly to the boil. Allow to boil for 10 minutes. Drain and peel the potatoes. Cut them into 2.5cm/1in cubes.
2. Deep-fry the potatoes in hot oil until lightly browned. Deep-fry the onions until golden-brown.
3. Heat the tablespoonful of oil in a frying pan or skillet. Fry the Maldive fish, if using, for about 30 seconds. Add the curry leaves, chilli powder and salt to taste and mix well. Lastly toss in the potatoes and the onions and stir. Remove from the heat. Just before serving, add the lime or lemon juice.

CAULIFLOWER BHAJI

Cauliflower is cooked in many different ways throughout India. This is my favourite. Care should be taken not to overcook the vegetable. The cooking time and quantity of water used depend on the size of the cauliflower florets.

SERVES 4

3–4 tablespoons oil
¼ teaspoon black mustard seeds
½ teaspoon cumin seeds
1 medium potato, cut into small dice
½ teaspoon ground cumin
½ teaspoon ground coriander
¼ teaspoon ground turmeric
*½ teaspoon garam masala (see page **31**)*
2 cloves of garlic, chopped
5 curry leaves
¼ teaspoon ground roasted cumin
2 green chillies, deseeded and chopped
salt
1 medium cauliflower, cut into florets
¼ cup water

To garnish
coriander leaves

1. Heat the oil in a saucepan over a low to medium heat. Add the mustard and cumin seeds, cover and allow to sputter for a couple of seconds over a low heat. Now add the potato and fry for 1 minute, stirring occasionally to prevent them from sticking to the pan. Add the ground cumin, coriander, turmeric, garam masala, garlic, curry leaves, roasted cumin, chillies and salt to taste and lastly the cauliflower. Stir until well mixed. Add the water and bring to the boil. Cover the pan and simmer for 5–7 minutes or until the cauliflower is cooked. Garnish with coriander leaves before serving.

STUFFED CAULIFLOWER

This is another unusual way of preparing a cauliflower. It looks attractive and tastes delicious, combining the flavours of coconut and spices.

SERVES 4

1 medium cauliflower
2 cups boiling water
¼ teaspoon ground turmeric
100g/4oz cooked peas
2 tablespoons desiccated coconut
juice of ½ lemon
1 teaspoon ground cumin
1 green chilli
salt

To serve
4 large lettuce leaves
1 tablespoon chopped coriander leaves

1. Remove any leaves and stalks from the cauliflower. Cut about 1cm/½in off the main stem so that the cauliflower can be stood upright when placed on a plate. Wash the cauliflower.
2. Put the boiling water into a saucepan large enough to hold the cauliflower. Add the turmeric. Place the cauliflower in the pan, bring to the boil and simmer for 10 minutes or until the cauliflower is just tender. Remove from the pan and leave to cool on a plate.
3. In a liquidizer, combine the peas, coconut, lemon juice, cumin, chilli and salt to taste. Blend to a smooth purée.
4. Place the cauliflower head downwards on a plate. Fill the crevices with the purée, making sure the cauliflower does not disintegrate.
5. Line a serving dish with the lettuce leaves. Carefully turn over the cauliflower to stand on its stem in the middle of the leaves. Sprinkle with coriander leaves.

ALU GOBI

(POTATO AND CAULIFLOWER DRY CURRY)

This recipe was given to me by a Bengali friend. In Bengal it is usual to add a little sugar to many spicy dishes.

SERVES 4

1 medium cauliflower
2 tablespoons oil
½ teaspoon black mustard seeds
100g/3½ oz potatoes, cut into 2.5cm/1in cubes
½ onion, finely chopped
¼ teaspoon ground turmeric
1 teaspoon ground cumin
1 teaspoon ground coriander
1½ teaspoons garam masala (see page **31***)*
2 teaspoons peeled and grated fresh root ginger
1 teaspoon sugar
salt
4 ripe tomatoes, chopped
½ cup water

1. Wash the cauliflower and cut it into even-sized florets. Cut the cauliflower stalks into 2.5cm/1in pieces.
2. Heat the oil in a medium saucepan. Add the mustard seeds, cover and allow to pop over a low heat. Add the potatoes and onion and fry until lightly browned. Add the turmeric, cumin, coriander and garam masala and fry for a couple of seconds. Now add the cauliflower florets and stalks and stir until well mixed. Add the ginger, sugar, salt to taste and the tomatoes with the water and bring rapidly to the boil. Lower the heat and simmer, covered, for 15 minutes.

ALU GOBI KARI

(CAULIFLOWER AND POTATO CURRY)

This cauliflower curry goes equally well with rice or chapatis.

SERVES 4

4 cloves of garlic
5 cm/2in piece of fresh root ginger, peeled
3 green chillies (optional), destalked
150ml/¼ pint cold water
2 tablespoons oil
1 medium onion, finely chopped
⅛ teaspoon ground black pepper
¼ teaspoon ground cardamom
¼ teaspoon ground turmeric
½ teaspoon ground coriander
1 teaspoon ground cumin
400g/14oz can of tomatoes
1 medium cauliflower, cut into even-sized florets
200g/7oz potatoes, cut into 2.5cm/1in cubes
salt

To garnish
coriander leaves

1. In a food processor, combine the garlic, ginger, chillies, if using, and water. Blend to a smooth paste.
2. Heat the oil in a medium saucepan and fry the onion until golden-brown. Add the pepper, cardamom, turmeric, coriander and cumin and fry for 30 seconds. Now add the ground paste and the tomatoes and stir until well mixed. Lastly add the cauliflower florets, potatoes and salt to taste, and bring to the boil. Cover and simmer for 15 minutes or until the potatoes are cooked. Garnish with coriander leaves before serving.

BONCHI KARI

(BEAN CURRY)

This is my version of a traditional Sri Lankan bean curry. If you cannot get hold of the fine Kenyan beans, any green beans can be used but the cooking time will have to be adjusted.

SERVES 4

225g/8oz fine Kenyan green beans
1 litre/1¾ pints water
2 tablespoons oil
¼ teaspoon black mustard seeds
6 curry leaves
1 small onion, finely chopped
1 teaspoon ground coriander
1 teaspoon ground cumin
¼ teaspoon ground turmeric
salt
1 tablespoon coconut milk powder

1. Wash the beans. Trim off the tops and tails and cut each bean into 2.5cm/1in pieces. (The cutting can be done quickly by holding the beans in bundles.)
2. Bring the water to the boil in a medium saucepan. Put in the beans and return rapidly to the boil, then boil rapidly for 2 minutes. Strain the beans and put into a bowl of cold water. (This helps them to remain crisp and retain their colour.
3. Heat the oil in a medium saucepan. Add the mustard seeds, cover and allow to pop over a low heat. Add the curry leaves and onion and fry until the onion is lightly browned. Drain the beans. Add the coriander, cumin and turmeric, toss in the beans and fry for 1 minute. Stir until well mixed. Add salt to taste and sprinkle the coconut milk powder on to the beans, taking care to stir thoroughly so that the milk powder does not become lumpy. Stir, cover and cook over a very low heat for 1 minute. The beans should be slightly crunchy and retain their green colour.

SPICY BEANS

This North Indian way of cooking beans is delicious provided they are not overcooked. The dish is eaten with chapatis and pooris but is equally good with rice.

SERVES 2

225g/8oz flat or runner beans
1½ tablespoons oil
¼ teaspoon mustard seeds
¼ teaspoon cumin seeds
½ medium onion, finely chopped
¼ teaspoon ground turmeric
½ teaspoon ground cumin
½ teaspoon ground coriander
salt
1 tablespoon water

1. Wash the beans and cut them into 1cm/½in pieces.
2. Heat the oil in a large saucepan. Add the mustard and cumin seeds, cover and allow to pop over a low heat. Add the onion and fry until lightly browned. Add the turmeric, cumin and coriander and stir for a couple of seconds. Add the beans and salt to taste and mix thoroughly. Add the water, cover and cook over a medium to high heat for about 5 minutes, until the beans are just cooked, stirring occasionally to ensure that they do not stick to the pan.

AVIAL

(MIXED VEGETABLE CURRY)

In this Kerala speciality vegetables are served in a coconut-flavoured yogurt sauce. Traditionally vegetables such as drumsticks (pods of the *Cassia fistula* tree which hang down from the branches in long, thin batons resembling drumsticks) and green bananas are used together with carrots and beans. You can use whatever combination of vegetables you like provided that you have a sufficient variety.

SERVES 4

200g/7oz carrots
200g/7oz sweet potato
200g/7oz fine green beans
500ml/118fl oz water
5cm/2in piece of fresh root ginger, peeled and chopped
3 green chillies, chopped
55g/2oz desiccated coconut
1½ teaspoons cumin
½ teaspoon ground turmeric
salt
425ml/¾ pint plain yogurt
1 tablespoon oil
10 curry leaves

1. Peel and wash the carrots and the sweet potato. Cut into 5cm/2in batons.
2. Wash the beans. Top and tail them, and cut each bean in half.
3. Bring the water to the boil in a medium saucepan. Add the turmeric and carrots and simmer for 5 minutes. Then add the sweet potato and beans. Return to the boil and simmer for a further 5 minutes, or until the vegetables are just cooked.
4. Put the ginger, chillies and coconut into a food processor or blender and blend until well mixed. Add to the vegetables. Add the cumin and salt to taste and simmer for a further 2 minutes. Stir until well mixed.
5. Add the yogurt and allow to heat through without boiling.
6. For the final seasoning heat the oil in a small saucepan. Add the curry leaves and allow to crisp up in the oil. Pour the oil and the leaves on to the vegetable stew. Stir and serve hot.

CABBAGE AND SPLIT PEAS

SERVES 4

125g/4oz split peas
3 cups boiling water
450g/1lb cabbage
2 tablespoons oil
¼ teaspoon black mustard seeds
1 teaspoon cumin seeds
8 curry leaves
2 whole dried red chillies
a pinch of asafoetida
¼ teaspoon ground turmeric
1 teaspoon ground cumin
salt

To garnish
coriander leaves

1. Soak the split peas in the boiling water for 2 hours, then drain.
2. Wash the cabbage and cut into 2.5cm/1in lengths, then chop roughly.
3. Heat the oil in a heavy-based frying pan or skillet. Add the mustard and cumin seeds and allow to sputter (care should be taken not to allow them to burn). Add the curry leaves, chillies and split peas. Stir-fry for 5 minutes. Add the asafoetida, turmeric and cumin, then add the cabbage, add salt to taste, and stir-fry over a low heat until the cabbage is cooked. Garnish with coriander leaves before serving.

MALLUNG

(SHREDDED GREENS)

This dish forms an integral part of a Sri Lankan rice-and-curry meal. A green leafy vegetable is shredded so finely as to make identification difficult. I have been known, on occasion, to make this recipe with both broccoli and brussels sprouts, thus confounding the taste-buds of my friends and family!

SERVES 2

225/8oz spring greens or cabbage
½ medium onion, chopped
½ teaspoon ground cumin
½ teaspoon ground black mustard
½ teaspoon ground coriander
¼ teaspoon ground turmeric
salt
2 tablespoons desiccated coconut
2 green chillies, finely chopped
1 tablespoon water

1. Wash and shred the greens or cabbage as finely as possible. (I use a food processor.)
2. In a large bowl combine the shredded greens or cabbage with all the remaining ingredients.
3. Stir-fry the greens or cabbage in a heavy-based frying pan or wok over a low heat for about 4 minutes. It should be barely cooked and should retain its green colour.

SHEBU BHAJI

(SPICY DILL)

If you like the flavour of dill you'll love this dish. Bunches of dill, available at Indian shops, are a lot cheaper than the dill available from supermarkets.

2 tablespoons oil
2 cloves of garlic, chopped
¼ teaspoon ground turmeric
1 teaspoon black mustard seeds
a pinch of asafoetida
1 dried red chilli
200g/7oz potatoes, boiled, cut into 2.5cm/1in cubes
200g/7oz dill, washed, trimmed and roughly chopped
salt

1. Heat the oil in a medium saucepan. Add the garlic and allow to brown over a low heat. Add the turmeric, mustard seeds, asafoetida and chilli, cover and allow the seeds to pop over a low heat. Now add the potatoes and stir until well mixed. Add the dill and salt to taste. Cook, covered, over a low heat for 5 minutes. The dill contains sufficient moisture to cook without the addition of any water.

SPICY MARROW

Since marrow contains a lot of water it is important to cook it over a high heat without any salt, which would draw out the water in the vegetable, making it mushy. The success of this dish is dependent on the marrow not being overcooked.

SERVES 4

1.35kg/3lb marrow
2 tablespoons oil
½ teaspoon cumin seeds
¼ teaspoon fenugreek seeds
¼ teaspoon ground turmeric
1 teaspoon ground coriander
*1 teaspoon ground roasted cumin (see page **28**)*
a pinch of asafoetida
2 tomatoes, peeled and chopped
5cm/2in piece of fresh root ginger, grated
1 tablespoon chopped coriander leaves

1. Wash the marrow and trim off the top and tail. Cut the marrow in half lengthwise, then cut each half in two again. Take one of the four segments and scoop away the seeds and pulp. Repeat for the remaining segments. Now cut the marrow into 2.5cm/1in cubes.
2. Heat the oil in a large saucepan. Add the cumin and fenugreek seeds, cover and allow to sizzle over a low heat. Add the turmeric, coriander, cumin and asafoetida. Add the marrow, increase the heat and stir-fry until the marrow is well coated in the spices. Add the tomatoes and ginger and mix well. Cover the pan and cook over a medium heat for 2 minutes or until the marrow is just cooked. Add the coriander leaves and serve immediately.

Stuffed Cauliflower

Vattakka Kari (Pumpkin Curry) with Red Rice

Haal Masso Badela (Fried Sprats) with Tomato and Onion Salad and Kosemberi

Goan Salmon Curry with Pol Sambal (Coconut Chutney) and Cucumber Raita

Jhinga Kari (Spicy Prawns) with Mallung (Shredded Greens)

Lamb Biriani

Saag Gosht (Lamb with Spinach)

Ooru Mus Kaluveta (Black Pork Curry) with Basmati Rice and Achcharu (Mixed Pickle)

COURGETTES (BABY MARROW OR ZUCCHINI)

Take care not to overcook the courgettes: they should have a 'bite' to them.

SERVES 4

450g/1lb courgettes
2 tablespoons oil
¼ teaspoon black mustard seeds
1 teaspoon ground cumin
1 medium onion, chopped
4 cloves of garlic, chopped
5 curry leaves
a pinch of ground turmeric
a pinch of asafoetida
2 green chillies, chopped
salt
3 tablespoons water

1. Wash the courgettes and cut them into 1cm/½in cubes.
2. Heat the oil in a medium saucepan. Add the mustard and cumin seeds, cover and allow to pop over a low heat. Add the onion, garlic and curry leaves and fry for about 2 minutes. Add the turmeric, asafoetida, chillies, and salt to taste and stir until well mixed. Add the courgettes and the water and stir-fry over a medium to high heat for 5 minutes or until the courgettes are cooked.

KARAVILA KARI

(CURRIED BITTER GOURD)

As its name implies, bitter gourd is really very bitter! By blanching the gourd in salted water and by adding gamboge to the dish the bitterness is somewhat reduced.

SERVES 4

225/8oz bitter gourd
salt
¼ teaspoon ground turmeric
½ teaspoon ground coriander
¼ teaspoon ground fenugreek
10 curry leaves
2 green chillies, chopped
1 onion, chopped
1 ripe tomato, chopped
3 tablespoons coconut milk powder
5 tablespoons water
2 pieces of gamboge
salt

1. Wash the bitter gourd. Cut each gourd in half lengthwise, then cut into 2.5cm/1in pieces.
2. Bring a saucepan of water to the boil. Add 1 teaspoon salt and the turmeric. Put in the gourd and bring back to the boil. Simmer for 5 minutes. Drain in a colander.
3. Combine the remaining ingredients in a medium saucepan and bring to the boil. Now add the blanched pieces of gourd and bring back to the boil. Cover and simmer for 5–7 minutes or until the gourd is cooked through.

NOTE: Gamboge is available in Sri Lankan and Indian shops and is known as *goraka* in Sinhala and *kokam* in Hindi.

DHUDHI KARI

(CURRIED BOTTLE GOURD)

This vegetable is readily available in Indian shops. It is eaten widely throughout India. You can also make it using butternut squash. Care should be taken not to overcook the squash.

SERVES 3–4

450g/1lb bottle gourd
2 tablespoons oil
½ teaspoon black mustard seeds
3 cloves of garlic, chopped
6 curry leaves
¼ teaspoon ground turmeric
⅛ teaspoon asafoetida
½ teaspoon ground cumin
½ teaspoon ground coriander
1 green chilli, chopped (optional)
1 tomato, roughly chopped
salt
100ml/3½fl oz water

To garnish
chopped coriander leaves

1. Wash the gourd. Peel it and cut into 1cm/½in cubes.
2. Heat the oil in a medium saucepan. Add the mustard seeds, cover and allow to sputter over a low heat. Add the garlic and curry leaves. Once the garlic is lightly browned, add the turmeric, asafoetida, cumin, coriander and the chilli, if using. Add the gourd cubes and stir until well mixed. Lastly add the tomato, salt to taste and the water and bring to the boil. Cover the pan and simmer for 10 minutes or until the gourd is soft but not overcooked. Garnish with coriander leaves and serve.

VATTAKKA KARI

(PUMPKIN CURRY)

In Sri Lanka large orange pumpkins are a popular vegetable. This is a traditional Sri Lankan preparation and has a delicious flavour.

SERVES 4

450g/1lb pumpkin
2 tablespoons desiccated coconut
5 cloves of garlic, chopped
½ medium onion, chopped
2 tablespoons cold water
1 teaspoon oil
¼ teaspoon black mustard seeds
a few curry leaves
1 teaspoon ground coriander
½ teaspoon ground cumin
¼ teaspoon ground turmeric
30g/1oz creamed coconut
1 cup hot water
salt

1. Wash the pumpkin. Peel off the skin and remove the seeds and the fibrous flesh around the seeds. Cut the pumpkin into 2.5cm/1in cubes.
2. Dry-roast the coconut in a heavy-based frying pan over a low heat until dark brown, stirring constantly to prevent the coconut from burning. In a food processor combine the garlic, onion and roasted coconut. Add the 2 tablespoons water and grind to a smooth paste.
3. Heat the oil in a medium saucepan. Add the mustard seeds, cover and allow to pop over a low heat. Add the curry leaves and the coriander, cumin and turmeric and fry for 30 seconds. Dissolve the creamed coconut in the hot water and add it to the pan together with the salt to taste. Add the ground coconut mixture and lastly add the pumpkin pieces. Bring to the boil, then simmer, covered, for 12–15 minutes, or until a skewer inserted into the pumpkin pierces it easily.

LEEKS IN GRAM FLOUR

SERVES 3

450g/1lb leeks
1 tablespoon oil
¼ teaspoon black mustard seeds
¼ teaspoon chilli powder
¼ teaspoon ground turmeric
salt
¾ cup water
30g/1oz gram flour

1. Wash the leeks thoroughly and cut them into 2.5cm/1in pieces.
2. Heat the oil in a saucepan. Add the mustard seeds, cover and allow to sputter over a low heat. Add the chilli powder, turmeric and salt to taste, then add the leeks. Toss the leeks in the pan for a few seconds. Add the water, bring to the boil and allow the leeks to cook over a low heat for about 5 minutes.
3. In a bowl, mix the flour with sufficient water to make a stiff paste. Remove the saucepan from the heat, and work the gram flour paste into the leeks. When thoroughly mixed, return to a low heat and allow to cook for 5 minutes.

LEEKS WITH WHITE CABBAGE

SERVES 4

225g/8oz leeks
225g/8oz white cabbage
2 tablespoons oil
¼ teaspoon black mustard seeds
½ teaspoon cumin seeds
2 whole red chillies
8 curry leaves
¼ teaspoon ground turmeric
a pinch of asafoetida (optional)
salt

1. Wash and finely shred the leeks and the cabbage.
2. Heat the oil in a large frying pan. Add the mustard and cumin seeds and allow to sputter (care should be taken not to allow them to burn). Add the chillies, curry leaves, turmeric and asafoetida and salt to taste and mix thoroughly. Add the cabbage and leeks and stir-fry over a medium heat for about 3–5 minutes.

MUSHROOM BHAJI

SERVES 4

450g/1lb mushrooms
3 tablespoons oil
4 cloves of garlic, chopped
2 medium onions, chopped
½ teaspoon ground turmeric
½ teaspoon ground chilli
1 teaspoon ground cumin
salt
juice of ½ lemon

1. Wipe the mushrooms and cut them into quarters.
2. Heat the oil in a saucepan and fry the garlic and the onions until lightly browned. Add the turmeric, chilli and cumin and stir for a couple of seconds. Lastly add the mushrooms and the salt to taste and stir-fry for a minute. Add the lemon juice before serving.

MOOLI BHAJI

(WHITE RADISH WITH COCONUT)

SERVES 4

450g/1lb white radish
2 tablespoons oil
¼ teaspoon black mustard seeds
1 medium onion, chopped
¼ teaspoon ground turmeric
a pinch of asafoetida
1 green chilli, chopped
salt
½ cup water

To garnish
30g/1oz desiccated coconut

1. Peel and wash the radish. Cut into strips 1cm/½in thick and 5cm/2in long.
2. Heat the oil in a saucepan. Add the mustard seeds, cover and allow to sputter over a low heat. Add the onion and cook until lightly browned. Add the turmeric, asafoetida, chilli and the radish and stir until well mixed. Add salt to taste and the water and simmer for about 5–7 minutes, until cooked. Garnish with the coconut before serving.

MALU MIRIS PURAVELA

(CURRIED STUFFED PEPPERS)

This is a popular accompaniment to a rice and curry meal in Sri Lanka.

SERVES 4

450g/1lb small green peppers (about 6)

For the stuffing
2 tablespoons oil
170g/6oz onions, finely chopped
2 teaspoons ground cumin
2 teaspoons ground coriander
½ teaspoon ground turmeric
½ teaspoon chilli powder
salt
400g/14oz potatoes, boiled and cubed

For the sauce
½ medium onion, finely chopped
6 cloves
6 cardamoms
2 cloves of garlic, finely chopped
2 teaspoons peeled and finely chopped fresh root ginger
salt
a few pieces of cinnamon stick
¼ teaspoon ground turmeric
½ teaspoon chilli powder
1 teaspoon ground coriander
1 teaspoon ground cumin
55g/2oz creamed coconut
1 cup water

1. Bring a large saucepan of water to the boil. Add the peppers and blanch for 5 minutes. Remove from the water, cut round the stems and remove the seeds.
2. To make the stuffing: heat the oil, add the onions and fry until softened in a small frying pan. Add the cumin, coriander, turmeric, chilli powder and salt to taste and mix thoroughly. Add the potatoes and mix thoroughly. Remove from the heat and allow to cool. Divide into 6 equal portions and fill each pepper with this spicy stuffing.
3. To make the sauce: combine all the ingredients and bring slowly to the boil. Lower the heat and simmer for 20 minutes. Add the stuffed peppers, arranging them so that they stand upright in the pan in a single layer, and cook over a low heat for a further 5 minutes until you have a thick coating sauce. Serve with rice.

ANNASI KARI

(PINEAPPLE CURRY)

In the southern region of Sri Lanka cubes of pineapple are pickled and also curried. The large round green pineapples from Costa Rica are best suited for the dish.

SERVES 6

1 large pineapple, not too ripe
3 tablespoons oil
1 medium onion, finely chopped
10 curry leaves
5cm/2in cinnamon stick
¼ teaspoon ground turmeric
1 teaspoon ground coriander
¼ teaspoon ground black mustard seeds
¼ teaspoon ground black pepper
1 teaspoon dried red chillies, coarsely ground
30g/1oz creamed coconut
200ml/7fl oz cold water
½ teaspoon ground roasted cumin
salt

1. Wash the pineapple and peel away the skin. Cut the pineapple in half lengthwise. Cut each half into 4 long strips. Cut off the central stalk and discard. Then cut the pineapple strips into 2.5cm/1in pieces.
2. Heat the oil and fry the onion, curry leaves and cinnamon over a medium heat until the onion is very lightly browned. Add the turmeric, coriander, mustard, pepper and chillies and stir until well mixed. Add the creamed coconut and the water and stir over a low heat for about 5 minutes, until the coconut has dissolved.
3. Add the pineapple and bring slowly to the boil. Simmer, uncovered, for 5 minutes. Just before serving sprinkle with the roasted cumin and salt to taste.

THAKKALI KARI

(TOMATO CURRY)

Fresh plum tomatoes are best suited for this dish, which is a speciality of Sri Lanka and is sometimes eaten with bread.

SERVES 4

450g/1lb firm, ripe tomatoes, chopped
1 tablespoon oil
½ medium onion, finely chopped
8 curry leaves
2 green chillies, chopped
1 teaspoon ground cumin
¼ teaspoon ground turmeric
1 teaspoon ground coriander
½ teaspoon ground chilli
1 tablespoon Maldive fish pieces (optional)
55g/2oz creamed coconut
salt
½ cup boiling water

1. Bring a saucepan of water to the boil. Put in the tomatoes for a couple of seconds. Remove from water and peel away the skins. Chop the tomatoes roughly.
2. Heat the oil in a saucepan over a low to medium heat and fry the onions and the curry leaves until the onions are lightly browned. Add the chillies, cumin, turmeric, coriander and chilli powder and stir until well mixed.
3. Add the tomatoes, the Maldive fish, if using, the creamed coconut and salt to taste. Add the water and stir until the coconut has dissolved. Simmer for 10 minutes.

LOONU KARI

(ONION CURRY)

This Sri Lankan dish is made with small red onions which are available in specialist stores. I have found that shallots or pickling onions are an equally good substitute.

SERVES 4

450g/1lb shallots or pickling onions
4 tablespoons coconut milk powder
200ml/7fl oz water
1½ teaspoons ground coriander
1 teaspoon ground cumin
¼ teaspoon ground turmeric
¼ teaspoon ground fenugreek
½ teaspoon chilli powder (optional)
½ tablespoon Maldive fish pieces (optional)
10 curry leaves
3 cardamom pods
5cm/2in cinnamon stick
salt
2 green chillies, chopped

1. Peel the onions and wash them in cold water.
2. In a medium saucepan, mix together the coconut milk powder and water. Add the remaining ingredients except for the onions and bring to the boil. Add the onions to this sauce. Bring back to the boil and simmer, covered, for 25 minutes, stirring occasionally.

NOTE: To make peeling shallots or small onions easier, pop them into a pan of boiling water for 30 seconds, then into a pan of cold water.

KAJU KARI

(CASHEW NUT CURRY)

When cashew nuts are in season in April, this Sri Lankan speciality is made using freshly picked nuts. By soaking cashews in bicarbonate of soda it is possible to recover the 'milky' flavour of the fresh nuts.

SERVES 4

1 teaspoon bicarbonate of soda
300g/10oz cashew nuts
2 tablespoons oil
½ medium onion, finely chopped
5cm/2in cinnamon stick
3 cloves
4 cardamom pods
¼ teaspoon ground turmeric
1½ teaspoons ground coriander
1 teaspoon ground cumin
salt
30g/1oz creamed coconut, chopped
225ml/8fl oz water

1. Put the bicarbonate of soda and 1 litre/1¾ pints cold water into a large bowl. Add the cashew nuts and soak for 4 hours, making sure that the nuts are immersed in the water.
2. Drain the cashew nuts and wash them in cold water.
3. Heat the oil in a medium saucepan over a low to medium heat. Add the onion, the cinnamon, the cloves and cardamom and fry until the onion is lightly browned. Add the turmeric, coriander, cumin and the nuts and stir until well mixed. Add the salt to taste, the creamed coconut and the water and bring to the boil. Lower the heat and cook, stirring from time to time, until most of the liquid has evaporated. This dish does not contain any sauce – the spice mixture should coat the nuts.

LENTILS AND VEGETARIAN DISHES

PARIPPU

(LENTIL CURRY)

Orange lentils cooked in coconut milk are eaten almost daily in Sri Lanka and South India.

SERVES 4

225g/8oz Mysore dhal (orange lentils)
3 cups water
1 medium onion, roughly chopped
55g/2oz creamed coconut
2 green chillies, chopped
¼ teaspoon ground turmeric
½ teaspoon ground cumin
½ teaspoon ground coriander
2 tablespoons oil
½ teaspoon cumin seeds
½ teaspoon black mustard seeds
1 onion, very finely chopped
10 curry leaves
salt

1. Pick over the lentils and wash them in several changes of cold water.
2. Put the lentils into a medium saucepan, together with the water. Add the roughly chopped onion, creamed coconut, chillies, turmeric, cumin and coriander and bring to the boil. Simmer and cook, uncovered, stirring occasionally, for about 25 minutes, until the lentils are a soft mush. If all the water has evaporated before the lentils are cooked, add a cup of boiling water.
3. While the lentils are simmering, heat the oil in a small saucepan. Add the cumin and mustard seeds, cover and allow the seeds to pop over a low heat. Add the finely chopped onion and curry leaves, and fry over a low heat until the onion is golden-brown.
4. Pour the onion mixture into the lentil mixture. Season to taste with salt and cook for a further 5 minutes. Serve hot with rice.

SARU

(SPICY LENTIL CURRY)

This lentil curry is from Karnataka. The spices for the curry are roasted before being ground. Because of the pepper and the chilli, it tends to be a little fiery.

SERVES 4–6

225g/8oz Mysore dhal (orange lentils)
2 ripe tomatoes, chopped
1 medium onion, chopped
1 litre/1¾ pints water
1 tablespoon coriander seeds
1 teaspoon cumin seeds
1 teaspoon black peppercorns
½ teaspoon fenugreek seeds
5cm/2in cinnamon stick
2 dried red chillies (optional)
10 curry leaves
1 teaspoon poppy seeds
2 tablespoons oil
¼ teaspoon black mustard seeds
¼ teaspoon ground turmeric
a pinch of asafoetida
salt

1. Pick over the lentils and wash them in several changes of cold water. Put the lentils, tomatoes and onion into a medium saucepan and add the water. Bring to the boil, then lower the heat and simmer for about 45 minutes, or until the lentils are cooked.
2. In a heavy-based frying pan, dry-roast the coriander, cumin, peppercorns, fenugreek, cinnamon, chilli, if using, and the curry leaves. As the poppy seeds are very fine they should be dry-roasted separately so that they don't burn. Grind all the roasted spices and the curry leaves to a fine powder (see page **20**) and add to the simmering lentils.
3. Heat the oil in a small saucepan. Add the mustard seeds, cover and allow the seeds to pop over a low heat. Add the turmeric, asafoetida and salt to taste. Pour this into the simmering lentils, and cook for a further 5 minutes. Serve with rice.

CHANA DHAL

This dhal has quite a nutty flavour and combines well with both rice and bread.

SERVES 4

225g/8oz chana dhal
5 cups cold water
1 medium onion, finely chopped
3 green chillies, chopped
1 teaspoon peeled and grated fresh root ginger
2 tablespoons oil
½ teaspoon ground coriander
½ teaspoon ground cumin
1 teaspoon garam masala (see page **31***)*
¼ teaspoon ground turmeric
1 teaspoon tomato purée
salt

1. Pick over the lentils and wash them in several changes of cold water. Soak the lentils for 2 hours in 3 cups of the water. Drain the lentils.
2. Put the lentils and the remaining water into a saucepan with the chillies, the ginger and half the onion. Bring to the boil, then cover and simmer for 50 minutes. Stir from time to time, and if the water has evaporated add ½ cup of boiling water. The lentils should be soft but not mushy when pressed between the thumb and forefinger.
3. Heat the oil in a small saucepan and fry the remaining onion until golden-brown. Add the coriander, cumin, garam masala, turmeric, tomato purée and salt to taste, and mix. Pour this spicy mixture into the lentils and bring back to the boil, then simmer for 5 minutes.

CHOLE CHAAT

(SPICY CHICKPEAS)

This chickpea preparation is sold at many a bazaar in the Indian sub-continent. In South India it is sold with cubes of diced coconut. It is an excellent accompaniment to any spicy meal.

SERVES 4

225g/8oz chickpeas
1.5 litres/2½ pints cold water
2 tablespoons oil
½ medium onion, finely chopped
1 teaspoon ground coriander
1 teaspoon ground cumin
¼ teaspoon ground turmeric
1 teaspoon garam masala (see page **31***)*
1 teaspoon grated, fresh root ginger
2 red chillies, chopped (optional)
200g/7oz canned tomatoes
salt

To garnish
coriander leaves

1. Pick over the chickpeas, then wash and soak in cold water for 10 hours, or overnight. Put the chickpeas and the 1.5 litres/2½ pints water into a saucepan and bring to the boil. Simmer for 1½ hours, or until the chickpeas are cooked. Take ½ cup of the chickpeas and mash them thoroughly. Reserve the whole chickpeas with the cooking liquid.
2. In another saucepan, heat the oil over a low heat. Add the onion and cook until golden-brown. Add the coriander, cumin, turmeric and garam masala and fry for 1 minute. Now add the ginger, chillies, if using, tomatoes and salt to taste, and stir until well mixed. Lastly add the whole chickpeas, their cooking liquid, and the mashed chickpeas. Bring to the boil, then lower the heat and simmer, uncovered, for 5 minutes. Garnish with the coriander leaves.

NOTE: Canned chickpeas are a less time-consuming substitute. Use 2 × 400g/14oz cans for this recipe. Drain off the water or the brine and proceed to stage 2 in the method.

DHAL SAAG

(LENTILS WITH SPINACH)

Mung lentils cooked with spinach form a traditional vegetarian dish. Serve with plain boiled rice and pickles.

SERVES 4

225g/8oz yellow mung lentils
570ml/1 pint cold water
2 green chillies
2–3 tablespoons oil
1 teaspoon black mustard seeds
8 curry leaves
¼ teaspoon asafoetida
¼ teaspoon ground turmeric
1 teaspoon ground cumin
1 teaspoon ground coriander
1 tablespoon peeled and grated fresh root ginger
salt
110g/4oz fresh spinach, roughly chopped
5 spring onions, finely chopped

1. Pick over the lentils and wash them in several changes of cold water. Put the lentils into a saucepan, add the water and bring to the boil. Lower the heat and simmer for 30 minutes, or until the lentils are mushy. The lentils will soak up most of the liquid during cooking.
2. Slit the chillies lengthwise, remove the seeds and cut the chillies into 1cm/½in pieces.
3. Heat the oil in a medium saucepan. Add the mustard seeds, cover and allow to sputter over a low heat. Add the curry leaves, asafoetida, turmeric, cumin and coriander. Add the ginger, chillies and salt to taste and stir into the cooked lentils until well mixed. Lastly add the spinach and spring onions, and cook over a low heat for about 2 minutes, or until the spinach is barely cooked.

GREEN LENTILS

Although these lentils have a brown husk, they are referred to as green lentils. They are delicious served with either rice or bread.

SERVES 4–6

225g/8oz green lentils
570ml/1 pint cold water
¼ teaspoon ground turmeric
5cm/2in piece of fresh root ginger, peeled and grated
a pinch of asafoetida
1 bay leaf
½ medium onion, roughly chopped
5cm/2in cinnamon stick
1 tablespoon tomato purée
2 tablespoons oil
½ teaspoon black mustard seeds
½ teaspoon cumin seeds
½ medium onion, finely chopped
1 dried red chilli (optional)
1 teaspoon ground coriander
1 teaspoon ground roasted cumin (see page **28***)*
1 teaspoon garam masala (see page **31***)*
salt

1. Pick over the lentils, wash them in several changes of cold water and soak them in cold water for 1 hour. Drain the lentils and place them in a saucepan, add the 570ml/1 pint water, the turmeric, ginger, asafoetida, bay leaf, roughly chopped onion, cinnamon and tomato purée and bring to the boil. Lower the heat and simmer for 30 minutes or until the lentils are cooked.

2. Heat the oil in a small saucepan. Add the mustard and cumin seeds, lower the heat and allow to pop over a low heat. Add the finely chopped onion and the chilli, cover and fry over a low to medium heat until the onion is golden-brown. Add the coriander, roasted cumin, garam masala and salt to taste. Pour the spicy mixture into the simmering lentils. Cook for a further 5 minutes.

SAMBAR

(VEGETABLE AND LENTIL STEW)

This is a South Indian vegetable and lentil preparation which is eaten with rice or dosa (see page **179**). Any combination of vegetables can be used, provided you make sure that the vegetables are cooked. Drumsticks, the pods of the *Cassia fistula* tree, are a vegetable used in both India and Sri Lanka. In Sri Lanka the leaves of the drumstick tree are used to flavour crab curries.

SERVES 4

225g/8oz thur dhal
2 tablespoons coriander seeds
10 black peppercorns
½ teaspoon fenugreek seeds
2 tablespoons desiccated coconut
1 tablespoon roasted chana dhal
6 dried red chillies
2 medium carrots, diced
2 drumsticks, cut into 5cm/2in pieces (optional)
1 onion, roughly chopped
110g/4oz aubergines, cubed
55g/2oz okra
30g/1oz tamarind
2 tablespoons oil
1 teaspoon black mustard seeds
10 curry leaves
½ teaspoon ground turmeric
½ teaspoon asafoetida
salt

1. Pick over the lentils, wash them in several changes of water and soak them in 2 cups of cold water for 2 hours.
2. Drain the lentils and place them in a saucepan with 1 litre/1¾ pints water. Bring to the boil, then cover, lower the heat and simmer for 2 hours or until cooked.
3. In a heavy-based frying pan, dry-roast the coriander seeds, peppercorns, fenugreek seeds, coconut, chana dhal and chillies over a low heat until the coconut is golden-brown. The mixture needs to be stirred constantly to prevent the coconut from burning. Grind the roasted mixture to a fine powder (see page **20**).
4. In a medium saucepan, bring 2 cups of water to the boil. Add the carrots and the drumsticks and bring back to the boil. Lower the heat and simmer for 10 minutes. Now add the onion, aubergine and okra, with more water if necessary. Simmer until the vegetables are almost cooked.
5. Put the tamarind into a saucepan together with a cup of water. Bring to the boil, then lower the heat and simmer for 15 minutes. Mash the tamarind with a fork. Put through a strainer and extract as much of the pulp as possible by pushing with the back of a spoon. Discard the fibres and reserve the strained pulp.
6. Put the cooked lentils, ground spices, vegetables (with any cooking water) and tamarind into a large saucepan and bring slowly to the boil. Lower the heat and allow to simmer.
7. Heat the oil in a small saucepan. Add

the mustard seeds, cover and allow to pop over a low heat. Add the curry leaves, turmeric, asafoetida and salt to taste. Pour on to the simmering lentils and stir until well mixed. Heat through thoroughly and serve.

KHATTE LOBIA

(BLACK-EYED BEANS)

It is the tamarind in this recipe that gives a tart flavour to the black-eyed beans. They are usually served with any of the Indian breads or with rice.

SERVES 4

225g/8oz black-eyed beans
30g/1oz tamarind
2–3 tablespoons oil
½ medium onion
1 teaspoon peeled and grated fresh root ginger
¼ teaspoon ground turmeric
½ teaspoon ground coriander
½ teaspoon ground cumin
5cm/2in cinnamon stick
salt

1. Pick over the black-eyed beans and wash them in several changes of cold water. Put them into a saucepan, add 2½ cups of cold water and bring to the boil. Lower the heat and simmer for about 30 minutes, or until the beans feel soft when pressed between the thumb and index finger. If the pan becomes dry, add ½ cup of water.
2. Soak the tamarind in ½ cup of water for about 1 hour. Put into a saucepan and bring to the boil, then lower the heat and simmer for 2 minutes. Put the tamarind through a strainer and extract as much of the pulp as possible. Reserve the water and discard the fibrous pulp.
3. In another saucepan, heat the oil over a medium heat. Add the onion and fry until lightly browned. Add the ginger, turmeric, coriander, cumin and cinnamon. Stir until well mixed. Lastly add the tamarind, beans and salt to taste. Mix thoroughly and simmer for 5 minutes.

MASALA RAJMA

(KIDNEY BEANS)

These spicy kidney beans are served with Indian bread. They need to be soaked for 8 hours before being cooked.

SERVES 4

225g/8oz kidney beans
3 tablespoons oil
½ medium onion, finely chopped
2 bay leaves
5cm/2in cinnamon stick
2 cloves of garlic
¼ teaspoon ground turmeric
½ teaspoon ground coriander
½ teaspoon ground cumin
½ teaspoon garam masala (see page **31***)*
3 dried red chillies
1 teaspoon peeled and grated fresh root ginger
salt

1. Pick over the kidney beans, wash them in several changes of cold water and put them into a large pan with 5 cups of cold water. Soak for 8 hours. Bring the beans to the boil in a saucepan, then lower the heat and simmer for about 1 hour or until tender.
2. Heat the oil in a saucepan, then lower the heat. Add the onion, bay leaves, cinnamon and garlic and cook until the onion is lightly browned. Now add the turmeric, coriander, cumin, garam masala, chillies, ginger and salt to taste. Stir until well mixed. Lastly put in the beans with whatever cooking liquid there is remaining in the pan. Bring to the boil and cook for a further 5 minutes, stirring constantly so that all the ingredients are well mixed.

OMELETTE CURRY

This egg preparation is characteristically Sri Lankan.

SERVES 4

4 tablespoons oil
1 medium onion, chopped
½ teaspoon peeled and finely chopped fresh root ginger
10 curry leaves
1 teaspoon ground coriander
¼ teaspoon ground fenugreek
1 teaspoon ground cumin
½ teaspoon chilli powder
30g/1oz creamed coconut
170ml/6fl oz water
salt

For the omelettes
6 eggs
½ medium onion, finely chopped
2 tomatoes, chopped
1 green chilli, finely chopped
salt
30g/1oz Maldive fish (optional)
oil for cooking

1. To make the gravy: heat the oil in a saucepan and fry the onion until golden-brown. Add the ginger, curry leaves, coriander, fenugreek, cumin and chilli. Fry for a couple of seconds. Add the creamed coconut, water and salt to taste and stir until the coconut has dissolved. Bring to the boil, then lower the heat and simmer for 5 minutes.
2. To make the omelettes: beat the eggs in a bowl, then add all the remaining ingredients. Heat a little oil in a heavy-based omelette pan. Add one-third of the egg mixture and cook until set. Fold in half and keep on a plate. Repeat the process until you have 3 omelettes. Cut each omelette into three. Bring the gravy to a slow boil, add the omelette pieces and simmer very gently for 5 minutes.

UNDEY KI KARI

(EGG CURRY)

This is a spicy way of serving hard-boiled eggs.

SERVES 4

6 eggs, hard-boiled and shelled
4 tablespoons oil
½ medium onion, finely chopped
5cm/2in cinnamon stick
4 cloves
3 cardamom pods
6 black peppercorns
2 bay leaves
¼ teaspoon ground turmeric
2 teaspoons ground coriander
1 teaspoon ground cumin
½ teaspoon garam masala (see page **31***)*
1 teaspoon grated fresh root ginger
2 green chillies, finely chopped
200g/7oz canned tomatoes
salt

To garnish
coriander leaves

1. Prick the eggs all over with a fork. Heat the oil in a frying pan and fry the eggs until lightly browned. Remove and drain on kitchen paper.
2. Reheat the oil and fry the onion until lightly browned. Add the cinnamon, cloves, cardamoms, peppercorns and bay leaves and fry for 30 seconds. Add the turmeric, coriander, cumin, garam masala, ginger, chillies, tomatoes and salt to taste and stir until well mixed.
3. Add the eggs and bring to the boil, then lower the heat and simmer, uncovered, for 2 minutes. Garnish with coriander leaves before serving.

SAAR

(SPICED YOGURT)

This buttermilk accompaniment is usually eaten with Kichiri (see page **43**) and is usually served in small individual bowls (*katoris*).

SERVES 2

200ml/7fl oz plain low-fat yogurt
2 tablespoons tomato purée
1 tablespoon oil
¼ teaspoon black mustard seeds
8 curry leaves
2 teaspoons peeled and grated fresh root ginger
¼ teaspoon ground turmeric
a pinch of asafoetida
salt

To garnish
30g/1oz coriander leaves, chopped

1. In a bowl, mix together the yogurt and tomato purée.
2. Heat the oil in a medium saucepan. Add the mustard seeds, cover and allow to pop over a low heat. Remove the lid and add the curry leaves, ginger, turmeric, asafoetida and salt to taste. Mix well. Pour in the yogurt and tomato mixture. Stir constantly over a low heat until almost boiling, then immediately remove from the heat to prevent the mixture from curdling. Serve in individual bowls, garnished with coriander leaves.

KHADI

(SPICED YOGURT)

This sauce is traditionally made from buttermilk and is eaten with Kichiri (see page **43**).

SERVES 4

350ml (12fl oz) plain unset low-fat yogurt
150ml (¼ pint) cold water
salt
1 teaspoon sugar
3 tablespoons gram (lentil) flour
2 tablespoons oil
1 teaspoon cumin seeds
10 curry leaves
¼ teaspoon ground turmeric
a pinch of asafoetida

1. In a bowl, whisk the yogurt with the water. Add salt to taste and the sugar.
2. In a small bowl, mix the gram flour with 2 tablespoons cold water.
3. Heat the oil in a medium saucepan. Add the cumin seeds, cover and allow to sizzle. Add the curry leaves, turmeric and asafoetida. Pour in the whisked yogurt and bring to the boil over a low heat. Add the gram flour paste, and simmer for 5 minutes, stirring constantly.

MATTAR PANIR

(CHEESE CURRY)

This is an excellent vegetarian dish that can be eaten with either rice or chapatis.

SERVES 4

For the cheese
1 litre/1¾ pints milk
juice of 1 large lemon
oil for deep-frying

For the curry sauce
2 tablespoons oil
½ teaspoon mustard seeds
1 medium onion, finely chopped
1 medium potato, cut into small cubes
2 teaspoons grated fresh root ginger
¼ teaspoon ground cumin
1 teaspoon ground coriander
½ teaspoon garam masala *(see page* **31***)*
½ teaspoon poppy seeds
1½ teaspoons tomato purée
1½ cups hot water
110g/4oz frozen peas
salt

To garnish
2 tablespoons chopped coriander leaves

1. Bring the milk to the boil in a saucepan. Add the lemon juice. The milk will curdle and the cheese will separate from the whey. Pour through a piece of muslin into a bowl and allow to drain. Squeeze out as much of the liquid as possible.

2. Put the milk solids in the muslin on to a clean work surface and knead thoroughly until smooth. Divide into 4 equal portions and shape each portion to form a cube. Deep-fry each piece in hot oil until golden-brown.

3. To make the curry sauce: heat the oil in a saucepan, add the mustard seeds, cover and allow to sputter over a low heat. Add the onion and fry until golden-brown. Add the potato cubes and fry until lightly browned. Add the ginger, cumin, coriander, garam masala and poppy seeds and fry for 30 seconds. Add the tomato purée, the water, peas and lastly the pieces of fried cheese. Add salt to taste and bring slowly to the boil. Simmer for 10 minutes, or until the potato is cooked. Garnish with coriander leaves before serving.

SEAFOOD

MALU CURRY

(SRI LANKAN FISH CURRY)

Fish is much more popular than meat in Sri Lanka, and there are many varieties of fresh fish available in the markets, ranging from the minuscule sprat to succulent seer fish which is steak-like in texture. Cooking fish in a spicy coconut sauce is the most popular preparation. I have chosen mackerel for this recipe as it is a firm fish which is well suited to currying.

SERVES 4

½ teaspoon fenugreek seeds
2 tablespoons hot water
2 pieces of gamboge
2 large mackerel, weighing about 1.5kg/3¼lb
1 lime or lemon
3 cloves of garlic, chopped
2 green chillies, chopped
5cm/2in piece of fresh root ginger, grated
1 teaspoon ground cumin
2 teaspoons ground coriander
¼ teaspoon ground turmeric
5 curry leaves
4 tablespoons coconut milk powder
100ml/3½fl oz cold water
salt

1. Soak the fenugreek seeds in the hot water. Wash the gamboge and set aside.
2. Cut off the mackerel heads and tails. Slit each mackerel about 3cm/1¼in along the belly and remove the entrails and any roe. Cut each mackerel into 4 cutlets, and without washing put into a large bowl. Squeeze the lime or lemon juice over the fish. Add the lime or lemon skins to the fish in the bowl and leave for 15 minutes. Wash each piece of fish quickly under cold running water and pat dry on kitchen paper.
3. In a wide pan large enough to hold the 8 pieces of mackerel in a single layer, combine the fenugreek, garlic, chillies, ginger, cumin, coriander, turmeric and curry leaves. Add the coconut milk powder and water, and mix thoroughly. Now add the mackerel, and carefully spoon over the spicy mixture to ensure that the fish is thoroughly coated. Bring to the boil over a medium heat and simmer for 15 minutes. Turn the pieces of fish over, add salt to taste, and cook for a further 7 minutes. Discard the pieces of gamboge and serve.

NOTE: I always wear a pair of disposable gloves when cleaning fish.

FISH IN YOGURT SAUCE

This delicately flavoured fish curry is mild and easy to prepare.

SERVES 4

1kg/2¼lb white fish fillets, preferably cod
4 tablespoons oil
2 medium onions, chopped
2 teaspoons peeled and chopped fresh root ginger
6 cloves of garlic, chopped
salt
¼ teaspoon ground turmeric
1 teaspoon ground cumin
2 teaspoons ground coriander
1 teaspoon garam masala *(see page* **31***)*
290ml/½ pint plain yogurt
4 green chillies, chopped

To garnish
coriander leaves

1. Wash the fish fillets and cut each in half.
2. Heat the oil in a wide pan large enough to hold the pieces of fish in a single layer, and fry the onions until lightly browned. Then add the ginger, garlic, salt to taste, turmeric, cumin, coriander and garam masala and fry for 2 minutes. Add the yogurt and the chillies and bring to just below boiling point. Simmer, covered, for 10 minutes. Slide in the pieces of fish and continue to simmer for 10–12 minutes or until the fish is cooked through. Garnish with coriander leaves and serve.

MACKEREL IN TAMARIND

Tamarind is widely used in the cuisine of Sri Lanka and India. It gives dishes a tangy quality and also acts as a preservative. Tamarind trees are large and provide shade from the sun.

SERVES 2

450g/1lb mackerel fillets
15g/½oz tamarind
1 cup water
1 tablespoon finely chopped fresh root ginger
3 cloves of garlic, finely chopped
½ teaspoon ground cumin
¼ teaspoon ground turmeric
¼ teaspoon ground coriander
1 teaspoon chilli powder
salt

1. Wash the mackerel in cold water and cut each fillet in half.
2. Soak the tamarind in 1 cup of water for 15 minutes. Put the tamarind and soaking water into a saucepan and bring to the boil. Simmer for 5 minutes. Strain the tamarind and reserve the water. Using the back of a metal spoon, press down to extract as much of the tamarind as possible. Discard the pulp.
3. Place the mackerel fillets in single layer in a shallow pan. Mix the ginger, garlic, cumin, turmeric, coriander, chilli powder and salt to taste with the tamarind water. Pour over the fish and bring to the boil over a medium heat. Cover and simmer for 10 minutes. Serve with boiled rice, vegetables and pickle.

HAAL MASSO BADELA

(FRIED SPRATS)

In Sri Lanka, many varieties of small fish are deep-fried and eaten as part of a meal. In Britain, the availability of small fish is much more limited, but when sprats are in season, I enjoy making this dish.

SERVES 4

450g/1lb fresh sprats
1 lime or lemon, cut into wedges
40g/1½oz plain white flour
½ teaspoon chilli powder
½ teaspoon ground black pepper
oil for deep-frying
salt

1. Cut off the sprat heads, slit each sprat about 2.5cm/1in along the belly and remove the entrails. Put the gutted fish into a large bowl without washing them. Squeeze the lime or lemon juice over the fish. Mix the lemon or lime skins into the fish and leave for 15 minutes. Then wash each sprat under cold running water and pat dry on kitchen paper.
2. Mix together the flour, chilli powder and pepper on a plate. Heat the oil over a medium heat. Dip each sprat in the seasoned flour and fry about 5 fish at a time for about 4 minutes or until evenly browned. Reheat the oil after each addition of fish. Allow the sprats to cool on a wire rack before draining on kitchen paper. Sprinkle with salt. They should be eaten whole, and should be crispy and crunchy.

AMBUL THIYAL

(SRI LANKA FISH IN GAMBOGE)

This is a typical fish preparation from the south of Sri Lanka. It is usually made with tuna and is always cooked in earthenware pots. It gets its distinctive flavour and preserving properties from the acidic gamboge. There is no liquid in the finished dish, which can be kept unrefrigerated for several days. Since mackerel is readily available in Britain, it can be used instead of tuna.

SERVES 4

30g/1oz gamboge
2 large mackerel, about 1.5kg/3¼lb
1 lime or lemon
4 large cloves of garlic
5cm piece of fresh root ginger, peeled
2 teaspoons coarsely ground red chilli powder (optional)
½ teaspoon black peppercorns
salt
100ml/3½fl oz water
5cm/2in cinnamon stick
10 curry leaves

1. Wash the gamboge and soak in a cup of water for 1 hour. Put the gamboge and water into a small saucepan and bring to the boil. Simmer for 15 minutes.

2. Cut off the heads and tails of the mackerel. Slit each mackerel about 3cm/1¼in along the belly and remove the entrails and any roe. Cut each mackerel into 4 cutlets and without washing put into a large bowl. Squeeze the lime or lemon juice over the fish. Add the lime or lemon skins to the fish in the bowl and leave for 15 minutes. Wash each piece of fish quickly under cold running water and pat dry on kitchen paper.

3. In a food processor combine the gamboge pieces, the garlic, ginger, chilli powder, if using, peppercorns and salt to taste. Add the water and blend to a smooth paste. Put the blended mixture into a wide pan large enough to hold the pieces of fish in a single layer. Add the fish and carefully turn the pieces over so that they are well coated. Add the cinnamon and curry leaves and bring to the boil. Carefully turn each piece of fish over, then cook, uncovered, for 20–30 minutes until all the liquid has evaporated.

GOAN SALMON CURRY

This salmon curry is spicy and hot! If you prefer a milder curry, deseed the chillies.

SERVES 4–6

6 dried red chillies
½ teaspoon ground turmeric
¼ teaspoon garam masala (see page **31***)*
1 tablespoon cumin seeds
1 teaspoon coriander seeds
1 teaspoon black mustard seeds
1kg/2¼lb salmon fillet, cut into serving-sized pieces

For the sauce
40g/1½oz tamarind
200ml/⅓ pint water
3 tablespoons oil
1 onion, thinly sliced
1 tomato, chopped
2 onions, finely chopped
8 cloves of garlic, chopped
6 green chillies, chopped
5cm/2in piece of peeled and grated fresh root ginger
salt
3 tablespoons coconut milk powder

1. Grind the dried chillies, turmeric, garam masala, cumin, coriander and mustard seeds to a fine powder (see page **20**).
2. To make the sauce: put the tamarind into a saucepan together with the water and bring slowly to the boil. Simmer for 10 minutes. Strain the tamarind into a bowl, pressing down with the back of a spoon to extract as much of the tamarind as possible. Discard the fibres and reserve the tamarind liquid.
3. Heat the oil in a wide pan large enough to hold the pieces of fish in a single layer. Fry the sliced onion until golden-brown. Add the tomato, the chopped onions, the garlic, chillies and ginger, and fry over a low to medium heat for about 20 minutes, or until the oil separates.
4. Add the ground spices, the tamarind water and salt to taste, and bring to the boil. Add the coconut milk powder and stir until well mixed. Lastly add the fish and bring slowly to the boil, then simmer for 5 minutes. Turn the pieces of fish over, and simmer for a further 5 minutes, or until the fish is cooked.

SRI LANKAN PICKLED TUNA

This fish preparation enables Sri Lankans who do not have refrigerators to cook in advance. Tuna is the only fish that is pickled in this way.

SERVES 4

450g/1lb fresh tuna
salt
¼ teaspoon ground black pepper
oil for deep-frying
5cm/2in piece of fresh root ginger, peeled
5 cloves of garlic
250 ml/9 fl oz wine vinegar
¼ teaspoon ground turmeric
½ teaspoon chilli powder
1 teaspoon ground black mustard seeds
½ teaspoon sugar

1. Wash the tuna and pat dry with kitchen paper. Cut it into 1cm/½ in slices. Season with salt and a little of the pepper.
2. Heat the oil and fry a few pieces of tuna at a time. Drain on a cooling rack.
3. Combine the ginger and garlic with the vinegar in a food processor and blend until smooth. Pour the purée into a saucepan and bring slowly to the boil. Add the turmeric, chilli, pepper, sugar and salt to taste. Bring back to the boil and simmer for 5 minutes. Remove from the heat and allow to become cold, then pour over the remaining fried fish. Store in a non-metallic container for up to 1 week, preferably in the refrigerator!

ISSO KARI

(PRAWN CURRY)

In coastal towns of Sri Lanka and South India, where shellfish and prawns are plentiful, this prawn curry cooked in coconut milk is a speciality. Fresh raw prawns (available in supermarkets) need to be shelled and deveined. Alternatively, use ready-cooked prawns which only require heating through in the sauce. Do not overcook prawns as they will become tough.

SERVES 4

450g/1lb prawns
juice of 1 lime
3 tablespoons oil
½ medium onion, chopped
½ teaspoon ground turmeric
½ teaspoon fenugreek seeds
5cm/2in cinnamon stick
5 curry leaves
1 teaspoon peeled and chopped fresh root ginger
3 cloves of garlic, chopped
55g/2oz creamed coconut
1 teaspoon chilli powder
150ml/¼ pint water
salt
juice of ½ lemon

1. Shell and devein the prawns. Put them into a bowl, add the lime juice and leave for 5 minutes. Wash each prawn under cold running water and pat dry with kitchen paper.
2. Heat the oil in a saucepan and fry the onion until lightly browned. Add the turmeric, fenugreek and cinnamon, the curry leaves, ginger and garlic, and fry for 1 minute. Add the creamed coconut, chilli powder, water and salt to taste, and bring slowly to the boil. Reduce the heat and simmer until the creamed coconut has dissolved. Add the prawns, bring back to the boil, and simmer for 5–7 minutes. Add the lemon juice and mix thoroughly.

NOTE: If using ready-cooked prawns, add them to the simmering sauce just prior to serving.

JHINGA KARI

(SPICY PRAWNS)

This prawn preparation takes a little time to prepare but is well worth the effort.

SERVES 2

400g/14oz raw shell-on prawns
juice of ½ lime
2 tablespoons fine desiccated coconut
2 ripe plum tomatoes
3 cloves of garlic
2.5cm/1in piece of fresh root ginger, peeled
½ medium onion
1 teaspoon fennel seeds
1½ teaspoons ground coriander
1 teaspoon ground cumin
⅛ teaspoon fenugreek seeds
1 teaspoon chilli powder
¼ teaspoon ground turmeric
2 tablespoons oil
10 curry leaves
100ml/3.5fl oz water
salt

To garnish
coriander leaves

1. Shell and devein the prawns. Put them into a bowl, add the lime juice and leave for 5 minutes. Wash each prawn under cold running water and pat dry with kitchen paper.
2. In a food processor, blend the coconut, tomatoes, garlic, ginger and onion to a purée.
3. Grind the fennel, coriander, cumin, fenugreek, chilli powder and turmeric to a fine powder (see page **20**).
4. Heat the oil in a medium saucepan. Add the curry leaves and ground spices and fry over a low heat for a couple of seconds. Add the blended ingredients and fry for a further 2–3 minutes. Add the water and bring slowly to the boil. Simmer for 2 minutes. Add the prawns and salt to taste and bring back to the boil. Simmer for 6–8 minutes, or until the prawns are cooked through. Garnish with coriander leaves and serve.

NOTES: If fresh plum tomatoes are unavailable, use canned tomatoes.

Care should be taken not to overcook the prawns.

DALLO KARI

(CURRIED SQUID)

Squid is very popular in Sri Lanka and is served curried, stuffed and sometimes fried. It has to be cooked only for a very short time or it will become rubbery.

SERVES 4

1kg/2¼lb fresh squid
1 teaspoon chilli powder
1 teaspoon ground cumin
1 teaspoon ground coriander
½ teaspoon ground turmeric
2 tablespoons oil
1 medium onion, finely chopped
10 curry leaves
½ teaspoon fenugreek seeds
4 cloves of garlic, finely chopped
5cm/2in piece of fresh root ginger, peeled and grated
4 tablespoons coconut milk powder
salt
170ml/6fl oz water
juice of 1 lime

1. Firmly grasp the squid head and tentacles and pull gently to separate the innards from the body sac. Remove the quill. Peel off the skin. Discard the head and tentacles. Wash the sac under cold running water, making sure that all the innards have been removed. Cut the squid into 2.5cm/1in wide rings.
2. In a bowl mix the squid with the chilli powder, cumin, coriander and turmeric.
3. Heat the oil in a medium saucepan and fry the onion until lightly browned. Add the curry leaves, fenugreek, garlic, ginger, coconut milk powder, salt and water. Bring slowly to the boil. Add the squid, and stir until well mixed. Simmer for 8–10 minutes. Add the lime juice and serve.

NOTE: Frozen squid is available from supermarkets but tends to be tough and needs longer cooking time.

MEAT AND POULTRY

MUS KARI

(BEEF CURRY)

This beef curry cooked in coconut milk is typically Sri Lankan.

SERVES 2

4 cardamom pods
½ teaspoon fennel seeds
4 cloves
5cm/2in cinnamon stick
¼ teaspoon fenugreek seeds
¼ teaspoon black peppercorns
3 tablespoons oil
1 medium onion, finely chopped
3 cloves of garlic, finely chopped
450g/1lb stewing beef, cut into 2.5cm/1in cubes
5cm/2in piece of peeled and finely chopped ginger, grated
¼ teaspoon ground turmeric
1½ teaspoons ground coriander
1 teaspoon chilli powder
55g/2oz creamed coconut, roughly chopped
1 cup hot water
salt

1. Grind the cardamom seeds, fennel, cloves, cinnamon, fenugreek and peppercorns to a fine powder (see page **20**).
2. Heat the oil in a flameproof casserole over a medium heat. Add the onions and garlic, and fry until lightly browned. Add the meat and fry until browned. Add the ginger and all the spices, and fry for 1 minute. Add the creamed coconut, water and salt to taste, and bring slowly to the boil. Stir until the creamed coconut has dissolved. Cover, lower the heat and simmer for about 1 hour, or until the meat is tender. If the liquid evaporates during the cooking time, add ½ cup of boiling water.

KEEMA

(MINCED LAMB)

This mild curry made with minced lamb and peas is a suitable dish to introduce children and adults alike to spicy food. It doesn't have much gravy and is usually eaten with one of the many Indian breads. I sometimes use it as a filling for toasted sandwiches.

SERVES 4

3–4 tablespoons oil
1 medium onion, finely chopped
2 cloves of garlic, finely chopped
450g/1lb minced lamb
2 teaspoons ground coriander
1 teaspoon ground cumin
¼ teaspoon ground turmeric
1 teaspoon garam masala (see page **31***)*
1 teaspoon peeled and grated fresh root ginger
2 green chillies, deseeded and finely chopped
2 teaspoons tomato purée
1 cup water
salt
110g/4oz fresh or frozen peas

To garnish
coriander leaves

1. Heat the oil in a saucepan and fry the onion until lightly brown. Add the garlic and the lamb and fry until the meat is lightly browned. Add the coriander, cumin, turmeric, garam masala, ginger and chillies, and fry for 1 further minute. Add the tomato purée, water and salt to taste and bring to the boil. Cover, lower the heat and simmer for about 45 minutes. If during the cooking time the liquid evaporates, add ½ cup boiling water.

2. Add the peas and cook for a further 10 minutes if fresh, 5 minutes if frozen. Garnish with coriander leaves before serving.

LAMB KORMA

I have enjoyed versions of this mild curry in both India and Malaysia. As a rule, it tastes better if made a day in advance. I usually add the lamb marrow bone to improve the flavour of the sauce. Very slow cooking is necessary for best results.

SERVES 2–3

450g/1lb leg of lamb, boned
2 medium onions
1 tablespoon plain yogurt
1 tablespoon desiccated coconut
1 tablespoon poppy seeds
2 green chillies, chopped
3 cloves of garlic
2.5cm/1in piece of fresh root ginger, peeled
30g/1oz cashew nuts
1 teaspoon ground cumin
2 teaspoons ground coriander
6 cloves
¼ teaspoon ground cinnamon
¼ teaspoon ground cardamom
2 tablespoons oil
salt

1. Cut the lamb into 2.5cm/1in cubes. Finely chop 1 onion and roughly chop the other. Put the cubed lamb in a bowl. Add the yogurt, mix thoroughly and set aside.
2. In a blender combine the roughly chopped onion and all remaining ingredients except for the thinly sliced onion, oil and salt. Blend to a smooth paste.
3. Heat the oil in a medium saucepan. Add the sliced onion and fry over a medium heat until lightly browned. Pour the mixture into the onion together with salt to taste, and cook over a low heat for 1 minute. Lastly, add the lamb and yogurt and bring slowly to the boil. Cover and simmer for 1½ hours, or until the meat is tender. If the water evaporates during cooking, add ½ cup boiling water. Stir the meat from time to time to prevent it from sticking to the pan.

LAMB KEBAB

SERVES 4

5 cloves of garlic
5cm/2in piece of fresh root ginger, peeled
3 green chillies
1 medium onion
3 tablespoons plain yogurt
3 tablespoons coriander leaves
450g/1lb minced lamb
½ teaspoon freshly ground black pepper
salt

To serve
lettuce leaves
onion rings
lemon wedges

1. Combine the garlic, ginger, chillies, onion, yogurt and coriander leaves in a food processor and process to a thick, smooth paste. Add the minced lamb, pepper and salt to taste, and process until well mixed. Divide into 16 equal portions. Shape each portion into a hamburger-type patty, place on a lightly oiled baking sheet and chill for 20 minutes.
2. Preheat the grill to high. Grill the lamb patties for 7 minutes or until browned on the top. Turn over and brown on the other side. Serve on a bed of lettuce with onion rings and lemon wedges.

NOTE: I sometimes make small lamb kebabs and put them on cocktail sticks to serve as an appetizer with drinks.

BOTI KEBABS

SERVES 4

675g/1½lb leg of lamb, off the bone
1 cup plain yogurt
3 teaspoons ground coriander seeds
½ teaspoon ground turmeric
1 teaspoon chilli powder
1 teaspoon freshly ground black pepper
1 teaspoon garam masala (see page **31***)*
salt

1. Cut the lamb into 2.5cm/1in cubes. In a large bowl, combine the yogurt, spices and salt. Add the cubes of meat and mix so that the meat is well coated in the marinade mixture. Leave, covered, for 6 hours in a refrigerator.
2. Thread the cubes of meat on to the skewers.
3. Preheat the grill to its highest setting. Place the skewers under the grill and cook for 5 minutes on each side. Lower the heat, brush the meat with the marinade mixture and cook for a further 5 minutes on each side. The cubes of meat should be nicely browned on the outside, but pinkish in the centre.

SAAG GOSHT

(LAMB WITH SPINACH)

This traditional North Indian lamb curry is made using mutton which requires slow boiling. If using lamb, reduce the amount of water to 290ml/½ pint, and adjust the cooking time accordingly. It is a dish without any gravy, and is delicious with either parathas (see page **55**) or any pulao rice.

SERVES 4

3 tablespoons oil
900g/2lb leg or shoulder of lamb, boned, trimmed and cut into 2.5cm/1in cubes
450g/1lb onions, finely chopped
6 cloves
6 cardamom pods
4 × 2.5cm/1in cinnamon sticks
10 black peppercorns
4 bay leaves
1½ teaspoons ground cumin
2 teaspoons ground coriander
*3 teaspoons garam masala (see page **31**)*
¼ teaspoon ground turmeric
1 teaspoon paprika
5cm/2in piece of fresh root ginger, peeled and grated
4 cloves of garlic, finely chopped
190ml (⅓ pint) plain yogurt
425ml/¾ pint water
salt
450g/1lb fresh spinach, washed and roughly chopped

1. Heat the oil in a medium saucepan over a low heat and fry the pieces of lamb a few at a time. Reserve. Add more oil to the pan if necessary, and fry the onions and the cloves, cardamoms, cinnamon, peppercorns and bay leaves. Cook until the onions are lightly browned. Now add the cumin, coriander, garam masala, turmeric and paprika and fry for a further 30 seconds. Add the lamb, ginger, garlic, yogurt, water and salt to taste, and bring to the boil. Cover, lower the heat and simmer for 2 hours. At this stage most of the water should have evaporated. If it has not, increase the heat and stir-fry until most of the moisture has evaporated.
2. Add the chopped spinach and cook for a further 3 minutes, until the spinach has wilted.

ROGAN JOSH

Perhaps the most famous Kashmiri dish, which gets its name from the red chillies used to give the characteristic colour.

SERVES 4

675g/1½lb leg of lamb, boned
4 tablespoons oil
4 bay leaves
6 cardamom pods
5cm/2in cinnamon stick
6 cloves
1 medium onion, finely chopped
4 cloves of garlic
5cm/2in piece of fresh root ginger, peeled
150ml/¼ pint plain yogurt
1 teaspoon fennel seeds
2 teaspoons ground cumin
2 teaspoons ground coriander
1 teaspoon chilli powder
200ml/7fl oz water
salt
½ teaspoon garam masala (see page **31***)*
4 teaspoons paprika

1. Cut the lamb into 2.5cm/1in cubes. Reserve any bones.
2. Heat the oil in a medium saucepan and fry a few pieces of lamb at a time until browned. Reheat the oil after each addition and add more oil if necessary.
3. Add the bay leaves, cardamom, cinnamon, cloves and onion to the pan and fry until the onion is lightly browned.
4. Blend the garlic, ginger, and yogurt in a food processor. Grind the fennel, cumin and coriander to a fine powder (see page **20**).
5. Add the ground spices to the onion in the pan. Add the lamb and any juices and stir until well mixed. Add the yogurt mixture, chilli powder, water and salt to taste, and bring slowly to the boil. Cover, lower the heat and simmer for 30–40 minutes.
6. Just prior to serving, add the garam masala and paprika and heat through.

NOTE: As Rogan Josh should be red in colour, I have found that it is best to add the paprika at the end of the cooking time to retain its redness.

KOFTA

(MEATBALL CURRY)

This traditional North Indian recipe for curried meatballs is made with minced lamb. However, it tastes equally nice using minced beef, and is never known not to please! It is versatile in that the sauce can also be used as a base for a vegetable curry, or even a fish curry.

SERVES 4

2 medium onions
450g/1lb minced lamb
3 cloves of garlic, finely chopped
1½ teaspoons peeled and grated fresh root ginger
2 green chillies, deseeded and finely chopped
salt
1 egg, beaten
3 tablespoons oil
4 × 2.5cm/1in cinnamon sticks
6 cloves
6 cardamom pods
2 teaspoons ground cumin
2 teaspoons ground coriander
½ teaspoon ground turmeric
1 teaspoon paprika
1 teaspoon garam masala (see page **31***)*
200g/7oz canned tomatoes
150ml/¼ pint plain yogurt

To garnish
coriander leaves

1. Grate 1 onion and finely chop the other. Put the grated onion into a sieve and with the back of a spoon press out as much of the liquid as possible. In a bowl, mix together the minced lamb, the grated onion, garlic, ginger, chillies, ½ teaspoonful of salt and the egg. Mix thoroughly. Divide the mixture into 20 equal portions and shape into balls. Cover with clingfilm and refrigerate for about 2 hours. Alternatively, the meatballs can be placed in the freezer while the sauce is being prepared, and they will then be sufficiently chilled to be slid into the sauce.

2. Heat the oil in a saucepan over a low to medium heat. Add the cinnamon, cloves, cardamom and the chopped onion, and fry until the onion is golden-brown. Add the ground cumin, coriander, turmeric, paprika, garam masala and salt to taste, and fry for 30 seconds or so. Add the tomatoes. Remove from the heat and slowly stir in the yogurt. Return to the heat, slide in the chilled meatballs and bring to the boil. Simmer, uncovered, for 1 hour over a very low heat. It may be necessary to shake the pan from time to time to prevent the meatballs from sticking. If during cooking the sauce runs dry, add ½ cup of water as required and continue to cook for the full hour. Garnish with coriander leaves before serving.

FRICCADELS

(CRISP-FRIED MEATBALLS)

These meatballs, which are Dutch in origin, are ideal to serve with drinks before dinner. They are usually included in a special packaged rice preparation called 'lumprice' which is made by the Dutch community in Sri Lanka.

SERVES 4

1 thick slice of stale white bread
½ cup of water
225g/8oz finely minced lean beef steak
2 cloves of garlic, finely chopped
1 teaspoon peeled and grated fresh root ginger
¼ teaspoon ground black pepper
2 green chillies, finely chopped
salt
1 egg, beaten
55g/2oz fine breadcrumbs
oil for deep-frying

1. Soak the slice of bread in the water for 10 minutes. Squeeze the water out by putting the slice of bread in a sieve and pressing down firmly with the back of a spoon.
2. In a large bowl, combine the bread together with all the remaining ingredients except the egg and breadcrumbs. Mix thoroughly. Divide into 16 equal portions and shape into balls. Refrigerate for 30 minutes.
3. Dip each meatball into the beaten egg, and coat in the breadcrumbs. Heat the oil over a low to medium heat. Fry a few meatballs at a time until golden-brown. Reheat the oil after each addition of meatballs. Remember that the meat is uncooked and if the oil is too hot, the outside will be burnt but the inside still raw. Drain on a cooling rack and serve hot.

NARGISI KOFTA

(SPICY SCOTCH EGG)

This North Indian speciality gets its name from the word *nargisi*, meaning 'narcissus'. The yellow and white of a boiled egg cut in half resembles the colours of the flower. This is very similar to a spicy Scotch egg, except that minced lamb is used in place of minced pork.

SERVES 4

½ medium onion, grated
500g/18oz finely minced lamb
1 tablespoon chopped mint leaves
1 tablespoon peeled and grated fresh root ginger
4 cloves of garlic
*2 teaspoons garam masala (see page **31**)*
½ teaspoon ground black pepper
salt
4 small eggs, hard-boiled and shelled
oil for deep-frying
1 egg, beaten
55g/2oz fine breadcrumbs

1. Put the onion into a sieve. Using the back of a metal spoon, press out as much of the liquid as possible.
2. Put the lamb, mint, onion, ginger, garlic, garam masala, pepper and salt to taste into a food processor, and blend until well mixed.
3. Divide the lamb mixture into 4 equal portions. Wet the palms of your hands and flatten each portion between the palms. Place a hardboiled egg in the centre of the lamb mixture and shape it round the egg, so that it becomes securely encased. Once all 4 eggs have been encased in this way, cover them with clingfilm and refrigerate for 30 minutes.
4. Heat the oil over a low to medium heat. Dip each kofta in beaten egg. Roll in the breadcrumbs and deep-fry over a low heat for 6–8 minutes. Since the lamb is raw the deep-frying should be done over a low heat to ensure that the meat is cooked right through. I usually fry only 2 koftas at a time as the oil temperature drops too much if all 4 are fried all at once. Drain the koftas on a cooling rack. Cut each kofta in half before serving.

OORU MUS KALUVETA

(BLACK PORK CURRY)

Sri Lankan curries are referred to as black when the spices used are dry-roasted before being ground. Pork curries are most popular amongst the Catholic community in Sri Lanka, and they are often made using wild boar, which has a delicious flavour.

SERVES 4–6

900g/2lb leg of pork
3 tablespoons oil
2 tablespoons coriander seeds
3 teaspoons cumin seeds
1 teaspoon fennel seeds
½ teaspoon ground turmeric
1 teaspoon chilli powder
55g/2oz tamarind
290ml/½ pint water
2 medium onions, finely chopped
5 cloves
5 cardamom pods
5cm/2in stick cinnamon
4 cloves of garlic, chopped
5cm/2in piece of fresh root ginger, peeled and grated
10 curry leaves
2 pieces of gamboge
4 tablespoons coconut milk powder
salt

1. Trim any excess fat from the pork and cut the meat into 2.5cm/1in cubes. Reserve any bones. Heat the oil in a frying pan and fry a few pieces of pork at a time, reheating the oil after each addition.

2. In a heavy-based frying pan, dry-roast the coriander, cumin and fennel over a low heat, until dark brown. Grind together with the turmeric and chilli powder (see page **20**).

3. Bring the tamarind and 100ml/3½fl oz of the water to the boil in a small saucepan. Simmer for 3 minutes. Put the tamarind into a fine strainer and, using the back of a metal spoon, press down to extract the pulp and juice. Reserve the water and the strained pulp and discard the fibres.

4. Reheat the oil in the pan, adding more if necessary to make up to about 4 tablespoons. Add the onions, cloves, cardamom and cinnamon, and fry until the onions are golden-brown. Add the garlic, ginger, the curry leaves and ground spices and fry for a couple of seconds. Add the pork and any bones, and the gamboge, and stir until well mixed. Lastly, add the tamarind, coconut milk powder, remaining water, and salt to taste, and bring slowly to the boil. Cover and simmer for 1 hour, or until the meat is tender.

PORK VINDALOO

Perhaps the most famous Goanese dish, introduced by the Portuguese. It is hot and fiery, and improves with keeping. *Vindaloo* comes from two words, *vind* meaning wine and *aloo* meaning garlic.

SERVES 4

1.4kg/3lb leg of pork, with bone
1 teaspoon black peppercorns
6 cardamom pods
4 dried red chillies
1 teaspoon cloves
4 × 2.5cm/1in cinnamon sticks
1 teaspoon cumin seeds
½ teaspoon ground turmeric
½ teaspoon ground coriander
¼ teaspoon fenugreek seeds
4 tablespoons red wine vinegar
1 tablespoon malt vinegar
4 green chillies
4 tablespoons oil
2 medium onions, thinly sliced
1 bulb of garlic, thinly sliced
5cm/2in piece of fresh root ginger, peeled and cut into matchsticks
3 ripe tomatoes, roughly chopped
1 cup of water
salt
1 teaspoon granulated sugar

1. Trim away the excess fat from the pork and cut the meat into 2.5cm/1in cubes. Reserve the bone.
2. Grind together the peppercorns, cardamoms, red chillies, cloves, cinnamon, cumin, turmeric, coriander and fenugreek (see page **20**).
3. In a large non-metallic container, mix the ground spices with the vinegars. Add the pieces of pork and mix thoroughly, making sure that all the pieces are coated in the spicy vinegar mixture. Cover and marinate for 3 hours.
4. Slit the green chillies in half lengthwise, then cut into 2.5cm/1in pieces.
5. Heat the oil in a saucepan and fry the onions until lightly browned. Add the garlic, ginger, tomatoes and chillies and stir until well mixed. Add the pork, increase the heat and fry for 3–5 minutes. Add the water and any of the marinade liquid left in the bowl, and bring slowly to the boil. Add salt to taste, the sugar and the bones, if using. Cover and simmer for about 1½ hours, stirring occasionally.

GOAN PORK BAFATH

This delicious Goanese dish tastes even better if it can be left for 24 hours after cooking. This recipe was given to me by my friend Sandra Lobo.

SERVES 4

2 tablespoons cumin seeds
2 tablespoons coriander seeds
1 teaspoon black mustard seeds
1 teaspoon ground turmeric
1 teaspoon chilli powder
900g/2lb lean shoulder of pork
salt
150ml/¼ pint malt vinegar
570ml/1 pint cold water
6 medium onions, roughly chopped
12 cloves of garlic, sliced
7cm/3in piece of fresh root ginger, peeled and cut into matchsticks
4 green chillies, slit lengthwise

1. Grind the cumin, coriander, mustard seeds, turmeric and chilli powder to a fine powder.
2. Trim any excess from the pork and cut the meat into 2.5cm/1in cubes. Put the pork together with the ground spices, salt and vinegar into a non-metallic container. Mix thoroughly. Marinate for at least 3 hours, turning the pork occasionally.
3. Transfer the pork to a large saucepan and add the water. Bring to the boil. Add the onions, garlic, ginger and green chillies. Cover and simmer for 2 hours.

KUKUL MUS KARI I

(SRI LANKAN CHICKEN CURRY)

Chicken curry is one of the highlights of a Sunday lunch in Sri Lanka. A distinctive flavour is imparted to it by the coconut milk and the roasted curry powder.

SERVES 4

1 quantity garam masala I (see page **31***)*
3 tablespoons oil
1 medium onion, finely chopped
450g/1lb skinned and boned chicken thighs, cut into bite-sized pieces
1 teaspoon peeled and chopped fresh root ginger
1 teaspoon chilli powder (optional)
salt
½ teaspoon ground turmeric
55g/2oz creamed coconut, roughly chopped
290ml/½ pint water

1. Heat the whole garam masala spices over a low to medium heat until they are lightly roasted. Shake the pan from time to time to ensure even roasting – if the spices are burnt the curry will taste bitter. Grind the spices to a fine powder (see page **20**).

2. Heat the oil in a medium saucepan and fry the onion until golden-brown. With a slotted spoon, remove the onions and reserve. Add the chicken, a few pieces at a time, adding more oil if necessary. Add the ground roasted spices, the onion and the remaining ingredients, except the creamed coconut and the water, and stir until well mixed. Lastly add the creamed coconut and the water, and bring rapidly to the boil. Stir until the creamed coconut is dissolved. Cover, lower the heat and simmer for about 1 hour or until the chicken is cooked.

NOTE: To vary the flavour of this curry you could omit the creamed coconut and add 150ml/¼ pint plain yogurt or 4 fresh or canned tomatoes instead. A combination of both yogurt and tomatoes is delicious.

KUKUL MUS KARI II

(SRI LANKAN CHICKEN CURRY)

This recipe takes a fair bit of preparation time, but is well worth the effort. In Sri Lanka a handful of soaked rice is ground along with the spices, but I have found that the sauce is sufficiently thick without adding the rice.

SERVES 4

3 tablespoons desiccated coconut
4 cloves of garlic
5cm/2in piece fresh root ginger, peeled
1 onion, roughly chopped
2 tablespoons coriander seeds
1½ teaspoons cumin seeds
1 teaspoon fennel seeds
1 teaspoon black peppercorns
8 cloves
12 cardamom pods
10cm/4in cinnamon stick
2 tablespoons oil
1 onion, finely chopped
10 curry leaves
900g/2lb chicken pieces
¼ teaspoon ground turmeric
1 teaspoon chilli powder (optional)
1½ cups of water
salt

1. In a heavy-based frying pan, over a low heat, dry-roast the desiccated coconut until golden-brown. It is important to keep stirring the coconut to prevent it from burning. Combine the coconut with the garlic, ginger, onion and ½ cup water in a food processor and grind to a smooth paste.

2. Dry-roast the coriander, cumin, fennel, pepper, cloves, cardamoms and cinnamon in the frying pan until lightly browned. Grind the roasted spices to a fine powder (see page **20**).

3. Heat the oil in a medium saucepan and fry the onion until lightly browned. Add the curry leaves and chicken, and cook for 1 minute, or until the chicken is brown on all sides. Add the ground roasted spices, the turmeric and chilli powder, if using, and the ground paste. Add 1 cup water and salt to taste and bring to the boil. Cover, lower the heat and simmer for 1 hour or until the chicken is cooked through.

KUKUL MUS MIRISATA

(SRI LANKAN RED CHICKEN)

In Sri Lanka curries are distinguished by their colour – red, black and white. This red chicken is fiery and hot. The hotness can be reduced by substituting paprika for the chilli powder in the recipe.

SERVES 4

8 chicken thighs, skinned, not boned
½ teaspoon ground black pepper
salt
500ml/18fl oz cold water
3–4 tablespoons oil
2 medium onions, finely chopped
20 curry leaves
8 cloves of garlic, finely chopped
5cm/2in piece of fresh root ginger, peeled and grated
3 teaspoons chilli powder
1 teaspoon paprika
2 teaspoons granulated sugar

1. Put the chicken, pepper and salt to taste into a saucepan with the water, and bring to the boil. Cover, lower the heat and simmer for 1 hour.
2. Remove the pieces of chicken to a plate. Bring the cooking stock rapidly to the boil and boil until reduced to about 150ml/¼ pint. Set aside.
3. Heat the oil in a medium saucepan. Add the onion and curry leaves, garlic and ginger, and fry until the onions are golden-brown. Add the chicken pieces and fry for a further 2–3 minutes. Add the chilli powder, paprika, sugar and chicken stock and bring slowly to the boil. Cover and simmer for 5–7 minutes, stirring occasionally to prevent the chicken from sticking to the pan.

MURGH KARI

(CHICKEN CURRY)

This subtle curry is North Indian in origin and is not hot.

SERVES 4

900g/2lb chicken quarters
1 teaspoon ground cumin
2 teaspoons ground coriander
1½ teaspoons garam masala (see page **31***)*
¼ teaspoon ground turmeric
2 medium onions
2 very ripe tomatoes
5cm/2in piece of fresh root ginger, peeled
4 cloves of garlic
3 tablespoons oil
5 cloves
8 cardamom pods
5cm/2in cinnamon stick
10 curry leaves
150ml/¼ pint plain yogurt
salt

To garnish
coriander leaves

1. Cut each chicken quarter in half. Mix together the cumin, coriander, garam masala and turmeric, and rub it into the chicken pieces.
2. Finely chop 1 onion and roughly chop the other. Chop the tomatoes, ginger and garlic. Put the roughly chopped onion, garlic, ginger and tomatoes into a food processor and blend to a smooth paste.
3. Heat the oil in a medium saucepan. Add the finely chopped onion, cloves, cardamom, cinnamon and curry leaves, and fry over a low to medium heat until the onions are golden-brown. Add the ground paste and stir for 5 minutes. Add the yogurt, spiced chicken and salt to taste and bring slowly to the boil. Cover, lower the heat and simmer for 50 minutes until the oil separates in the gravy. Stir occasionally to prevent the chicken from sticking. Garnish with coriander leaves and serve.

TANDOORI CHICKEN

Traditionally this dish is cooked in the *tandoori* clay oven. It is a very popular dish in North India and is always served on a bed of salad with onion rings and lemon wedges and is eaten with naan (see page **53**). You have to plan to make it a day in advance.

SERVES 4

1 chicken, about 1.5kg/3¼lb
1 medium onion, chopped
3 cloves of garlic, chopped
5cm/2in piece of fresh root ginger, peeled and chopped
190ml/⅓ pint plain yogurt
grated zest and juice of 1 lemon
2 tablespoons vinegar
1 teaspoon paprika
*2 teaspoons garam masala (see page **31**)*
2 teaspoons ground coriander
1 teaspoon ground cumin
½ teaspoon red food colouring (optional)
*2 tablespoons ghee (see page **32**)*

To serve
lettuce leaves
onion rings
cucumber slices
lemon wedges

1. Remove the skin from the chicken and cut it in half. Using a sharp knife, make slanting incisions 2.5cm/1in long in the chicken on the legs and breast, taking care not to cut right through to the bone.

2. Combine all the remaining ingredients except the chicken and ghee in a food processor and grind to a smooth paste.

3. Put the paste in a large non-metallic bowl. Add the chicken and marinate for 8–24 hours. Turn the chicken occasionally in the marinade.

4. Preheat the oven to 200°C/400°F/gas mark 6. Place the chicken on a wire rack or a baking tray. Cover with foil and roast on the top shelf of the preheated oven for 45 minutes, basting the chicken with the marinade mixture once during cooking. Remove the foil and cook for a further 15 minutes until the chicken is browned.

5. Prior to serving, heat the ghee, pour over the chicken halves and ignite. Serve the chicken on a bed of lettuce garnished with onion rings, cucumber slices and lemon wedges. Serve with naan.

NOTE: The marinated chicken pieces can also be grilled, barbecued or spit-roasted.

Kukul Mus Mirisata (Sri Lankan Red Chicken)
with Annasi Kari (Pineapple Curry) and Pappadams

Clockwise from top: *Lemon Pickle; Green Coriander Coconut Chutney; Seeni Sambal; Date Chutney*

Dhokla (Steamed Lentil Cubes)

Clockwise from top: *Stuffed Parathas (Stuffed Fried Unleavened Bread); Roti (Coconut Bread); Dosa (Pancakes); Methi Poori (Deep-fried Unleavened Bread with Fenugreek Leaves)*

Pakoda (Vegetables in Lentil Batter)

Clockwise from top: *Malu Cutlis (Fish Balls); Devilled Cashew Nuts; Patties*

Sri Lankan Love Cake with Mango Mousse

Jalebi with Gulab Jamun

CHICKEN TIKKA MASALA

This dish was created in London and can be loosely translated to mean pieces of chicken in spices. Since ready-to-use tikka pastes are available in jars in most supermarkets, I have found it unnecessary to make my own! It is best to marinate the chicken overnight, so you have to plan to make this dish a day in advance.

SERVES 4

450g/2½lb chicken breasts, skinned
2½ tablespoons tikka paste
juice of ½ a lemon
4 cloves of garlic
5cm/2in piece of fresh root ginger, peeled
15g/½oz coriander leaves
100ml/3½fl oz plain yogurt
salt

1. Cut the chicken into 2.5cm/1in cubes.
2. Put the remaining ingredients into a food processor and blend until smooth.
3. Put the chicken pieces into a non-metallic bowl. Add the blended ingredients and mix thoroughly. Cover and leave overnight in the refrigerator.
4. Preheat the oven to 200°C/400°F/gas mark 6.
5. Put the marinated chicken pieces on to a baking tray and cook, uncovered, in the middle of the preheated oven for 15–20 minutes, or until the chicken is cooked.

NOTE: The chicken can also be grilled. I sometimes leave the chicken breasts whole and barbecue them. Because the tikka paste contains salt, very little extra salt is needed.

KASHMIRI CHICKEN

This mild chicken dish combines spices and nuts.

SERVES 3–4

1 chicken, about 1.5kg/3¼lb
½ cup chicken stock (see page **33***)*
2 tablespoons ghee or oil
1 medium onion, finely chopped
4 cloves of garlic, finely chopped
1 teaspoon peeled and finely chopped fresh root ginger
½ teaspoon ground cinnamon
½ teaspoon ground coriander
½ teaspoon ground cumin
¼ teaspoon ground black pepper
½ teaspoon ground cloves
½ teaspoon ground cardamom
55g/2oz ground almonds
55g/2oz ground pistachio nuts
225ml/8fl oz yogurt
½ teaspoon saffron powder, dissolved in 1 teaspoon hot water
salt

1. Remove the skin from the chicken. Using a sharp knife, cut away as much of the flesh as possible from the carcass. Cut the chicken into bite-size pieces and reserve the carcass for making stock (see page **33**).
2. Heat the ghee or oil in a saucepan and fry the onion until golden-brown. Add the garlic, ginger and chicken and fry rapidly for about 5 minutes. Add the cinnamon, coriander, cumin, pepper, cloves, cardamom and chicken stock and simmer for 30 minutes.
3. Blend the ground nuts with the yogurt. Add to the pan with the saffron liquid and salt to taste, and bring to the boil. Simmer for 10 minutes before serving.

KASHMIRI CHICKEN LIVERS

Another speciality from the northern Indian province of Kashmir, where Moorish influences have blended with the culinary traditions of the sub-continent.

SERVES 2

225g/8oz frozen chicken livers
3 tablespoons oil
2 medium onions, finely chopped
3 cloves of garlic, chopped
1 tablespoon cumin seeds
1 teaspoon chilli powder
1 tablespoon peeled and grated fresh root ginger
½ teaspoon ground turmeric
salt
1 cup water

1. Slice the chicken livers when partially defrosted.
2. Heat the oil in a medium saucepan over a medium heat. Add the onions and cook until transparent. Add the garlic and cumin seeds and fry for 1 minute. Add the chilli, ginger, turmeric and salt. Add the chicken livers, turn the heat up slightly and stir-fry for 2–3 minutes. Add the water and bring to the boil, then cover, lower the heat and simmer for 15–20 minutes.

SALADS, CHUTNEYS AND PICKLES

RADISH SALAD

This salad combines radishes with peanuts and takes only minutes to make. The dressing should be added just prior to serving, as the salt and lemon juice tend to draw the water from the radishes.

SERVES 4

310g/11oz radishes
1 tablespoon oil
¼ teaspoon cumin seeds
¼ teaspoon mustard seeds
a pinch of asafoetida
⅛ teaspoon ground turmeric
½ teaspoon salt
1 tablespoon lemon juice
110g/4oz peanuts, roasted

1. Wash the radishes and top and tail them. Cut each radish in half lengthwise and place in a bowl.
2. Heat the oil in a small saucepan. Add the cumin and mustard seeds, cover and allow to pop over a low heat. Add the asafoetida, turmeric and salt. Remove from the heat and add the lemon juice. Pour the mixture on to the radishes. Add the peanuts, toss until well mixed and serve immediately.

NOTES: To roast the peanuts preheat the oven to 170°C/325°F/gas mark 3. Place the peanuts on a baking sheet and roast in the centre of the oven for 30 minutes. Allow to cool. The skins should then come off easily as each nut is rubbed between the thumb and index finger.

Alternatively, add 100g/3½oz of ready-salted peanuts and remember to reduce the salt by half.

CARROT SALAD

This carrot salad is popular throughout India.

SERVES 4

450g/1lb carrots
1 tablespoon oil
¼ teaspoon black mustard seeds
¼ teaspoon cumin seeds
⅛ teaspoon ground turmeric
salt
juice of ½ lemon

To garnish
coriander leaves

1. Wash and peel the carrots and grate them finely.
2. Heat the oil in a small saucepan. Add the mustard and cumin seeds, cover and allow to pop over a medium heat. Add the turmeric and the salt to taste. Remove from the heat and allow to cool for 5 minutes. Add the lemon juice. Mix well, then toss into the carrots and mix thoroughly. Garnish with coriander leaves before serving.

KOSEMBERI

This salad combines raw soaked lentils with grated carrots or radishes and has an unusual texture. Remember to soak the lentils well in advance.

SERVES 4

55g/2oz yellow mung lentils
200g/7oz carrots or white radish, grated
30g/1oz freshly grated coconut, or desiccated coconut
30g/1oz coriander leaves, washed and chopped
2 tablespoons oil
½ teaspoon black mustard seeds
2 red chillies, broken into pieces (optional)
salt
2 tablespoons lemon juice

1. Pick over the lentils and wash them in several changes of cold water. Soak the lentils in plenty of cold water for 3 hours, then drain in a sieve.
2. In a bowl, combine the lentils, the grated carrot or radish, coconut and coriander leaves.
3. Heat the oil in a small saucepan. Add the mustard seeds, cover and allow the seeds to pop over a medium heat. Add the chillies, remove from the heat, and add the salt and lemon juice. Allow to cool completely, then pour over the salad ingredients and toss thoroughly before serving

TOMATO AND ONION SALAD

This is a popular Sri Lankan salad which is usually made with red onions.

SERVES 4

225g/8oz red onions, thinly sliced
juice of 1 lemon
2 green chillies, finely chopped
¼ teaspoon ground black pepper
salt
225g/8oz beef tomatoes, thinly sliced

1. In a bowl, combine the onions with the lemon juice, chillies, pepper and salt to taste, cover and leave for at least 1 hour.
2. Just prior to serving, mix in the sliced tomatoes.

LETTUCE WITH PEANUT DRESSING

This salad has an unusual combination of textures.

SERVES 4

½ iceberg lettuce
1 cucumber
2 ripe tomatoes
55g/2oz peanuts, coarsely ground
4 tablespoons oil
¼ teaspoon black mustard seeds
¼ teaspoon cumin seeds
¼ teaspoon ground turmeric
a pinch of asafoetida
½ teaspoon salt
2 tablespoons lemon juice

1. Wash the lettuce, cucumber and tomatoes and drain thoroughly. Slice the cucumber and roughly chop the tomatoes. Combine the salad ingredients in a bowl. Add the peanuts.
2. Heat the oil in a small saucepan. Add the mustard and cumin seeds, cover and allow to pop over a medium heat. Add the turmeric, asafoetida and salt to taste. Remove from the heat, add the lemon juice and allow to cool completely.
3. Just prior to serving, toss the salad with the dressing.

CUCUMBER RAITA

This is a cooling and refreshing accompaniment to a hot, spicy meal. It can also be served as a dip.

SERVES 4

225g/8oz cucumber
½ teaspoon salt
290ml/½ pint Greek yogurt
2 tablespoons chopped mint
¼ teaspoon ground black pepper

1. Wash the cucumber and pat dry with kitchen paper. Grate the unpeeled cucumber and sprinkle with the salt. Drain the grated cucumber in a strainer or piece of muslin, pressing out as much of the water as possible.
2. In a bowl, combine the yogurt, mint and pepper. Just prior to serving, add the drained, grated cucumber.

DATE CHUTNEY

This sweet and sour chutney not only is the perfect accompaniment to a spicy meal, but also tastes delicious in cheese sandwiches.

SERVES 8

170ml/6fl oz malt vinegar
3 tablespoons brown sugar
140g/5oz chopped dried dates
2 cloves of garlic, finely chopped
1 teaspoon peeled and finely chopped fresh root ginger
30g/1oz sultanas
1 teaspoon paprika
salt

1. Put the vinegar and sugar into a saucepan and bring slowly to the boil. Stir until the sugar has dissolved. Lower the heat and add the dates, garlic and ginger. Cook over a low heat for 15 minutes, stirring all the time. Add the sultanas, paprika and salt to taste and cook for a further 5 minutes.
2. Put into jars and store. Once opened, store in the refrigerator for up to a month.

TOMATO CHUTNEY

This chutney is best made when tomatoes are in season and have been naturally ripened in the sun.

SERVES 8

1.5kg/3¼lb firm, ripe tomatoes
1kg/2¼lb onions, finely chopped
1kg/2¼lb granulated sugar
100g/3½oz soft dark brown sugar
15g/½oz peeled and finely chopped fresh root ginger
salt
7g/¼oz chilli powder
570ml/1 pint malt vinegar

1. Put the tomatoes into a pan of boiling water for 30 seconds. Remove and immerse in a bowl of cold water. Peel off the skins. Roughly chop the tomatoes.
2. Put all the ingredients, except the vinegar, into a heavy-based saucepan. Bring slowly to the boil and stir until the sugar has dissolved. Cook for about 1 hour, stirring occasionally, until most of the liquid has evaporated and the mixture is fairly thick and the tomatoes almost caramelized.
3. Add the vinegar and cook for another 10 minutes until thick and syrupy. Pour the chutney, while hot, into dry, sterile jars. Seal and store in a cool, dry place.

NOTE: For best results use fresh Italian plum tomatoes.

POL SAMBAL

(COCONUT CHUTNEY)

This hot chutney is typically Sri Lankan, combining the grated kernel of the coconut with hot chilli powder.

SERVES 4

110g/4oz freshly grated coconut
1 teaspoon coarse chilli powder
salt
¼ teaspoon ground black pepper
3 small red onions, or 2 shallots
3 cloves of garlic
juice of 1 lime

1. Combine all the ingredients in a food processor and blend until well mixed.

NOTES: Small red onions are available in Chinese supermarkets.

Unsweetened desiccated coconut can be substituted for freshly grated coconut. Finely chopped spring onions can be added to make an interesting variation.

GREEN CORIANDER COCONUT CHUTNEY

This coriander chutney can be served with dosa (see page **179**) or any unleavened bread. Although referred to as a chutney, it is more of a sambal. The term *chutney* comes from a Hindi word meaning 'to be licked'. Chutneys are usually made from acidic fruits with onions, dates and raisins, and seasoned with spices and vinegar. In India and Sri Lanka the word is used loosely to describe any relish which is eaten in small quantities with rice or snacks. *Sambal* comes from a Malay word, and is used to refer to any relish that can be either cooked or uncooked, for example Pol Sambal (see page **161**) and Seeni Sambal (see page **166**).

SERVES 6

30g/1oz tamarind
1 cup boiling water
200g/7oz unsweetened desiccated coconut
55g/2oz coriander leaves
55g/2oz roasted split gram
4–6 green chillies, chopped
salt

1. Soak the tamarind in the boiling water for 10 minutes. Put the tamarind and the soaking liquid into a small saucepan, and bring slowly to the boil. Cover, lower the heat and simmer for 5 minutes.
2. Strain the tamarind pulp, pressing down with the back of a spoon to extract as much of the tamarind as possible. Discard the pulp and reserve the strained tamarind.
3. Put the coconut, coriander leaves, roasted gram, chillies, salt to taste and the tamarind into a food processor, and blend until smooth. If the mixture seems dry, add a couple of tablespoons of water during the blending. Store, covered, in the refrigerator for up to 1 week.

NOTE: Roasted split gram is available in Indian supermarkets.

MINT SAMBAL

This is a delicious accompaniment to any spicy meal.

SERVES 4

55g/2oz fresh mint leaves
½ teaspoon freshly ground black pepper
15g/½oz onions
¼ teaspoon sugar
2 green chillies, roughly chopped
2.5cm/1in piece of fresh root ginger, peeled and chopped
salt
juice of ½ lime

1. Wash the mint in several changes of water.
2. Put all the ingredients into a food processor and grind to a smooth paste.

KARAVILA SAMBOLA

(BITTER GOURD SAMBAL)

Karavila, once deep-fried, tends to lose some of its bitterness. It has long been believed that this vegetable has special medicinal properties. Considered to be of especial help for diabetics, it can even be bought in tablet form.

SERVES 4

225g/8oz bitter gourd, about 2 fruits
salt
2 cups water
oil for deep-frying
1 medium onion, thinly sliced
2 green chillies, chopped
1½ teaspoons malt vinegar
¼ teaspoon ground mustard seeds
1 tablespoon coconut milk powder

1. Wash the bitter gourds. Cut off the stems and stalks. Using a very sharp knife, cut each bitter gourd into thin, even slices (about the thickness of potato crisps). Put 1 teaspoon salt into the water and soak the bitter gourd slices for 30 minutes. Drain and pat dry with kitchen paper.
2. Heat the oil until it is almost smoking hot. Deep-fry the bitter gourd slices, a few at a time, taking care not to over-crowd the pan, as the slices need to fry comfortably on the surface of the oil. After about a minute, turn the bitter gourd slices over, and fry for a further minute or until dark brown. Take care not to burn the gourd. Drain on kitchen paper. Repeat until all the gourd is fried.
3. Just prior to serving, combine the onion, chillies and gourd slices in a salad bowl. In a small bowl mix together the vinegar, salt to taste, the mustard and the coconut milk powder. Pour over the gourd and mix thoroughly.

DRIED PRAWN SAMBAL

This dried prawn relish is an extremely tasty accompaniment to all rice dishes. Somewhat less savoury is the lingering smell of fish which the slow cooking of the dried prawns tends to leave! I usually take the precaution of sealing off the kitchen from the rest of the house by firmly shutting all connecting doors, as well as opening all the kitchen windows. However, it is, I believe, a small penalty to pay for a dish that never fails to be a success.

SERVES 6

55g/2oz dried prawns
225g/8oz onions
3 cloves of garlic, chopped
oil for deep-frying plus extra oil
½ teaspoon peeled and grated fresh root ginger
½ teaspoon chilli powder
salt
2 teaspoons lemon juice

1. Preheat the oven to 100°C/200°F/gas mark ½. Wash the prawns and pat dry with kitchen paper. Place in a roasting pan and put them into the oven for 1 hour. Grind the prawns in a blender.
2. Slice the onions thinly and chop the garlic. Heat the oil and deep-fry the onions a few at a time until golden-brown. Drain on kitchen paper.
3. Heat 1 tablespoon oil in a small saucepan, and fry the garlic until lightly browned. Add the prawn powder and fry over a very low heat for about 3 minutes. Add the ginger, chilli powder, onions and salt to taste, and mix thoroughly.
4. Remove from the heat, add the lemon juice and serve.

SEENI SAMBAL

This is a Sri Lankan speciality and is relished as an accompaniment to any rice and curry meal. It is eaten in small quantities, and loosely translated means 'sugar sambal' despite the many other ingredients that go to make it.

SERVES 6

oil for deep-frying plus 1 tablespoon
675g/1½lb onions, thinly sliced
15g/½oz tamarind
1 cup water
1½ teaspoons Maldive fish or dried prawns, coarsely ground
4 cloves of garlic, finely chopped
1½ teaspoons peeled and finely chopped fresh root ginger
10 curry leaves
30g/1oz creamed coconut, dissolved in ½ cup boiling water
1 tablespoon chilli powder
1 teaspoon sugar
4 cardamom pods
2 × 2.5cm/1in cinnamon sticks
salt

1. Heat the oil and deep-fry the onions, a few at a time, until golden-brown. Drain on kitchen paper.
2. Soak the tamarind in the water for about 20 minutes. Put the tamarind and the soaking water into a saucepan and cook over a low heat for about 5 minutes. Strain the tamarind and, using the back of a metal spoon, press firmly to extract as much of the tamarind as possible. Discard the fibrous pulp and reserve the strained tamarind.
3. Heat the tablespoon of oil in a small saucepan, and add the Maldive fish or prawns. Fry for about 5 minutes. Add the garlic and the ginger, then all the remaining ingredients, including the tamarind water and the onions. Bring to the boil, then simmer over a very low heat until the liquid evaporates.

LUNUMIRIS

(HOT ONION SAMBAL)

This is a popular Sri Lankan accompaniment, particularly to rotis (see page **54**), hoppers and Kiribath (see page **39**).

SERVES 4

225g/8oz shallots or small red onions
1 teaspoon coarsely ground chilli powder
1 teaspoon lime or lemon juice
salt
½ tablespoon Maldive fish

1. Peel the shallots and wash them thoroughly. Combine the shallots, chilli powder, lime or lemon juice and salt to taste in a food processor. Blend until the onions are ground. Add the Maldive fish. Mix and serve.

NOTE: Small red onions, available in Chinese supermarkets, are best suited for this dish.

LEMON PICKLE

A sour pickle that goes well with any spicy meal.

SERVES 10

450g/1lb lemons
2 cups water
½ teaspoon ground turmeric
2 tablespoons salt
½ teaspoon fenugreek seeds
1 teaspoon mustard seeds
1 tablespoon chilli powder
2 tablespoons oil

1. Wash the lemons. Place them in a saucepan with the water and turmeric, and bring to the boil. Boil for 7 minutes, then drain.
2. On a plate, cut each lemon into 8 sections. Remove the pips. Sprinkle with the salt and store in a dry jam jar for 1 week, turning the lemons every day.
3. In a heavy-based frying pan, over a low heat, lightly brown the fenugreek and mustard seeds, taking care not to let them burn. Allow to cool, then grind to a powder (see page **20**). Mix the mustard, fenugreek and chilli powder into the lemons. Pour the oil over the top of the lemons to act as a seal. Store in a cool, dry place.

ACHCHARU

(MIXED PICKLE)

This pickle is usually made using small red onions, available in Chinese and other supermarkets. It can be eaten with any spicy meal and is also delicious with cold meat.

SERVES 10

225g/8oz french beans
225g/8oz carrots
225g/8oz red onions or pickling onions
55g/2oz green chillies
290ml/½ pint water
150ml/¼ pint malt vinegar
¼ teaspoon ground turmeric
½ teaspoon salt

For the pickling paste
150ml/¼ pint malt vinegar
3 cloves of garlic, peeled
5cm/2in piece of fresh root ginger, peeled
1 tablespoon freshly ground black mustard seeds
1 teaspoon chilli powder
salt
2 teaspoons sugar

1. Begin by preparing the vegetables. Top and tail the beans and cut them into 5cm/2in pieces. Peel the carrots and cut into 5cm/2in sticks. Peel the onions. Wash the chillies. Bring the water and vinegar to the boil in a saucepan. Add the turmeric and salt. Blanch the beans for 2 minutes. Remove, and bring the water back to the boil. Add the carrots and boil for 3 minutes. Remove, bring the water back to the boil, then blanch the onions for 3 minutes. Remove, and lastly blanch the chillies for 2 minutes. Leave all the vegetables to drain in a colander. (Leave the pan covered during blanching to minimise evaporation.)
2. To make the pickling paste: put the vinegar, garlic and ginger into a food processor and blend until the garlic and ginger are finely ground. In a large mixing bowl, combine this mixture with the mustard, chilli powder, sugar and salt to taste, and mix thoroughly. Add the drained vegetables, and stir until evenly coated. Put into 3 clean, dry jam jars and cover tightly. Store in a cool, dry place.

NOTE: I always store the jars on their sides so that the vinegar makes maximum contact with the blanched vegetables. Once opened, the pickle can be stored in the refrigerator for a month.

SNACKS

PAPPADAMS

Packaged pappadams are excellent and are easy to prepare. They are made with lentil flour and rice flour and are sometimes flavoured with chilli, garlic, pepper or cumin. They can be deep-fried, microwaved, or 'roasted' on a gas hob.

SERVES 4

1 packet pappadams
oil for deep-frying

1. Using a pair of scissors, cut each pappadam into 4 equal pieces.
2. Heat the oil until hot. Put in a pappadam quarter. In a matter of seconds it will expand and rise to the surface. Turn over and fry for 1 second. The frying should be done very quickly to prevent the pappadams from burning.
3. Drain on a cooling rack before drying on kitchen paper.

NOTES: Pappadams can be prepared very successfully in a microwave oven. Microwave on full power, one at a time, for 50–60 seconds, depending on their size. They crisp up as they cool.

SAMOSAS

Samosas are the most popular Indian savoury snacks and can contain a spicy meat or vegetable filling.

SERVES 8

For the dough
225g/8oz plain flour
salt
4 tablespoons oil
about 5 tablespoons tepid water

For the filling
2 tablespoons oil
½ medium onion, finely chopped
½ teaspoon ground coriander
½ teaspoon ground cumin
¼ teaspoon ground turmeric
½ teaspoon garam masala (see page **31***)*
400g/14oz boiled potatoes, cut into small dice
2 green chillies, chopped
1 tablespoon peeled and chopped fresh root ginger
salt
55g/2oz cooked peas
1 teaspoon cumin seeds
½ teaspoon ground roasted cumin seeds
juice of ½ lemon

1. To make the dough: sift the flour and salt into a bowl. Dribble in the oil and rub it in with your fingers until the mixture resembles breadcrumbs. Add the water a little at a time and mix to a dough with a palette knife. Put the dough on a floured surface and knead for 5 minutes until smooth and pliable. Cover and leave at room temperature for 15 minutes. Do not refrigerate as the oil will congeal, making the pastry difficult to roll.

2. To make the filling: heat the oil in a saucepan. Add the onion and fry until lightly browned. Add the coriander, cumin, turmeric and garam masala. Add the potatoes, chillies, ginger and salt to taste and stir for a minute or two, making sure the mixture does not stick to the bottom of the pan. Add the cumin seeds, roasted cumin and lemon juice and mix thoroughly. Leave to cool.

3. On a floured surface, roll out one-third of the pastry to a circle about 27.5cm/11in. (The pastry should be roughly 3mm/⅛in thick.) Using a 7.5cm/3in cutter, cut circles of pastry. Place ½ tablespoon of the filling in the centre of each circle of pastry. Moisten the edges with a little water and seal to give a semi-circular shape. Repeat the process until all the filling has been used up. Leave the samosas covered until ready to fry.

4. Heat the oil over a medium heat. Add a small piece of pastry and when it rises to the surface within a couple of seconds, the oil is ready for use. Put in a few samosas at a time, and fry until lightly browned. Turn over and allow to brown on the other side. Remove and place on a cooling rack for 5 minutes before placing on kitchen paper. Once cold, store in an airtight container in the refrigerator for up to 3 days.

MALU PAN

(SPICY BREAD ROLLS)

Rolls filled with a spicy meat, fish, or onion filling are a popular snack in Sri Lanka.

SERVES 8

For the dough
750g/1lb 10oz strong white flour
1 teaspoon salt
1 sachet easy-blend dried yeast
55g/2oz margarine
about 400ml/14fl oz tepid water
a little milk for brushing

For the filling
1 × 400g/14oz can mackerel in brine
150g/5oz potatoes, boiled and peeled
2 tablespoons oil
½ medium onion, finely chopped
2 green chillies, finely chopped
5cm/2in piece of fresh root ginger
2 cloves of garlic, finely chopped
1 teaspoon ground cumin
1 teaspoon ground coriander
⅛ teaspoon ground turmeric
1 teaspoon chilli powder
2 tablespoons coconut milk
juice of ½ lemon
salt

1. To make the dough: sift the flour into a bowl. Add the salt and yeast. Rub in the margarine until the mixture resembles fine breadcrumbs. Gradually add enough water to mix to a soft, pliable dough.
2. Knead the dough on a lightly-floured surface until smooth and elastic.
3. Leave the dough covered in a bowl until doubled in volume.
4. Meanwhile, make the filling: put the mackerel into a colander and leave to drain for 10 minutes.
5. Remove the skin and bones from the mackerel fillets. Using a fork, roughly mash the mackerel together with the potatoes.
6. Heat the oil in a saucepan, and sweat the onion. Add the chillies, ginger and garlic, then the cumin, coriander, turmeric and chilli. Add the fish and potatoes, and stir until well mixed. Add the coconut milk powder, lemon juice and salt to taste. Remove from the heat and allow to cool on a plate.
7. Punch the dough down and divide into 16 equal portions. Flatten each portion to a 12.5cm/5in circle. Put a tablespoonful of the filling in the centre of each circle, draw up the edge to form a pouch, and seal. Leave on a greased baking tray to prove for about 30 minutes.
8. Preheat the oven to 200°C/400°F/gas mark 6. Brush the rolls with milk and bake in the oven for 13–15 minutes, until risen and lightly browned. Cool on a rack.

KACHORIS

(STUFFED UNLEAVENED PASTIES)

These stuffed unleavened pooris take some time to make but are well worth the effort. Traditionally they are circular in shape but I find it easier to make them semi-circular.

SERVES 4

For the dough:
100g/3½oz wholemeal flour
100g/3½oz plain flour
salt
1 teaspoon kalonji (black onion seeds)
2 teaspoons oil
140–170ml/5–6fl oz tepid water
oil for deep-frying

For the filling
100g/3½oz urad dhal (split white lentils)
1 cup water
1 tablespoon oil
1 teaspoon cumin seeds
¼ teaspoon ground turmeric
¼ teaspoon asafoetida
3 green chillies, finely chopped (optional)
2 teaspoons peeled and grated fresh root ginger
salt

1. Pick over the dhal and wash it in several changes of water, then soak in cold water for 2 hours. Strain and put the dhal into a food processor or blender together with the water, and grind the dhal coarsely.

2. To make the dough: mix the flours and salt together in a bowl and add the kalonji seeds. Dribble in the oil, and add sufficient water to form a soft, pliable dough. Knead the dough for 3 minutes, then cover and leave at room temperature for about 30 minutes.

3. To make the filling: heat the oil in a medium saucepan over a medium heat. Add the cumin seeds, cover and allow to sputter. Add the turmeric, asafoetida, chillies and ginger. Stir until well mixed. Lastly, add the coarsely ground lentils and salt to taste. Add the water and cook over a low heat until the liquid has evaporated, stirring to prevent the mixture from sticking to the pan. Spread the mixture on a plate and leave to get cold.

4. Take a quantity of dough about the size of a walnut and roll it out to resemble a thin pancake about 7.5–10cm/3–4in in diameter. Place 1 teaspoonful of the lentil mixture in the centre of the dough. Now fold over to form a semi-circle. Pinch the edges to seal securely. Roll out on a floured surface, taking care to apply gentle pressure so that the filling doesn't ooze out. Try to retain the semi-circular shape of the *kachori*.

5. Heat the oil until it is hot. Add the *kachori* and when it rises to the surface, gently press it down with a metal spoon to submerge it in the oil. This encourages the *kachori* to puff up. Turn over and cook for a couple of seconds on the other side. Drain and repeat the process until you have used up all the dough.

SHOMSHA

(COCONUT PASTIES)

These mini coconut-filled pastries from Bengal are eaten as a snack.

SERVES 6–8

For the dough
225g/8oz plain flour
4 tablespoons oil
about 5 tablespoons tepid water
oil for deep-frying

For the filling
100g/3½oz granulated sugar
200ml/7fl oz water
2 bay leaves
5cm/2in cinnamon stick
100g/3½oz desiccated coconut
¼ teaspoon ground cardamom

1. To make the dough: sift the flour into a bowl. Dribble in the oil and rub it in with your fingers until the mixture resembles breadcrumbs. Add the water a little at a time and mix to a dough with a palette knife. Put the dough on a floured surface and knead for 5 minutes until it is smooth and pliable. Cover and leave at room temperature for 15 minutes. Do not refrigerate as the oil will congeal, making the dough difficult to roll.

2. To make the filling: put the sugar, water, bay leaves and cinnamon into a heavy-based saucepan. Heat gently until the sugar has dissolved. Bring to the boil and add the coconut. Stir and cook over a low to medium heat until the liquid has evaporated and the mixture comes together. It should not be bone-dry. Remove from the heat, add the cardamom and allow to cool.

3. On a lightly floured surface, roll out one-third of the pastry to a circle about 27.5cm/11in. Using a 7.5cm/3in cutter, cut out circles of pastry. Place ½ tablespoon of the filling in the centre of each circle of pastry. Moisten the edges with water and seal to give a semi-circular shape. Repeat the process until all the filling has been used up. Cover the shomshas and leave until ready to fry.

4. Heat the oil over a medium heat. Add a small piece of pastry: when it rises to the surface in a couple of seconds, the oil is ready for use. Put in a few shomshas at a time and fry until lightly browned. Turn over and allow to brown on the other side. Remove and place on a cooling rack for 5 minutes before placing on kitchen paper. Once cold, store in an airtight container for up to a week.

DHOKLA

(STEAMED LENTIL CUBES)

A Gujerati steamed snack made with gram flour. It is flavoured with coriander leaves, lemon juice and freshly grated coconut. It should be light and spongy.

SERVES 4

125g/5oz gram flour
salt
1 tablespoon oil
½ teaspoon bicarbonate of soda
½ teaspoon citric acid powder
100ml/3½fl oz water, plus 2 teaspoons water

For the pouring sauce
2 tablespoons oil
½ teaspoon black mustard seeds
¼ teaspoon ground turmeric
3 green chillies, chopped
2 teaspoons sugar
juice of ½ lemon

To garnish
a handful of coriander leaves
30g/1oz freshly grated coconut, or desiccated coconut

1. Bring about 5cm/2in water to the boil in a steamer or large saucepan with a colander large enough to contain a deep 15cm/6in square dish.

2. Sift the flour into a bowl. Add salt to taste, the oil and the bicarbonate of soda. Dissolve the citric acid in the 2 teaspoons water. Pour the citric acid and the 100ml/3½fl oz water into the flour and mix thoroughly with a wooden spoon to form a batter. Pour into the greased dish, cover securely with oiled greaseproof paper, and steam for 20 minutes, or until a skewer inserted comes out clean. Cut the dhokla into diamond-shaped pieces.

3. To make the pouring sauce: heat the oil in a small saucepan. Add the mustard seeds, cover and allow to pop over a medium heat. Add the turmeric, chillies, sugar, lemon juice and salt to taste. Remove from the heat and pour over the steamed dhokla. Garnish with coriander leaves and coconut.

DOSA

(PANCAKES)

You have to plan to make dosas 2 days in advance as the mixture has to be left to ferment. Dosas are a South Indian speciality and are always eaten with coconut chutney (see page **162**), potatoes cooked with tamarind (see page **180**) and samba (see page **105–6**). Hard to describe to the uninitiated, they most closely resemble savoury pancakes. For flour and eggs, read rice and dhal!

MAKES ABOUT 25

100g/3½oz urad dhal (split white lentils)
200g/7oz long-grain patna-type rice
295ml/10½fl oz cold water
salt
oil for cooking

1. Pick over the dhal and wash it and the rice separately in several changes of water. Soak both the rice and the dhal overnight in separate bowls of cold water.
2. Drain the dhal and put into a food processor. Add 200ml/7fl oz of the water and grind to a smooth paste. Put the ground dhal into a large bowl. Now drain the rice. Put the rice into the food processor, add the remaining water and grind until smooth. The rice takes much longer to grind than the dhal. Add the rice to the ground dhal, add salt to taste, and mix thoroughly. Cover and leave overnight to ferment.
3. Heat a griddle or a heavy-based pan. Lightly grease the surface with a teaspoon of oil. Pour 2 tablespoons of the dosa mixture into the centre of the hot griddle. Using the back of a metal spoon, quickly spread the mixture very thinly over the surface of the griddle. The quicker this spreading is done, the thinner the dosa will be. Take a teaspoon of oil and dribble over the dosa. This helps to crisp it up. I like making paper-thin dosas so I don't turn them over. If the mixture has not been spread very thinly in the first instance, turn the dosa over and cook for 30 seconds on the other side as you would for a pancake. Dosas are best eaten as soon as they are cooked.

NOTE: Sometimes chopped onions and chillies are mixed into the fermented dough, which is made into thick pancakes and served for breakfast. They are called *uttapam*. Sometimes the dosas are filled with spicy potatoes as well (see following recipe).

POTATO FILLING FOR DOSA

The tamarind gives this potato dish its unique South Indian flavour and it is always served as a filling for dosas.

SERVES 4–6

30g/1oz tamarind
300ml/11fl oz water
3 tablespoons oil
1 teaspoon black mustard seeds
10 curry leaves
¼ teaspoon ground turmeric
2 green chillies, chopped
a pinch of asafoetida (optional)
200g/7oz onions
600g/1¼lb potatoes, cut into 1cm/½in cubes
salt

1. Put the tamarind into a saucepan with the water and bring to the boil. Simmer for 5 minutes. With a fork, mash the tamarind while hot. Strain the tamarind, pressing down with the back of a spoon to extract as much of the liquid as possible, and discard the fibrous pulp.
2. Heat the oil in a medium saucepan. Add the mustard seeds, cover and allow to pop over a low heat. Add the curry leaves, turmeric, chillies and asafoetida, if using. Add the onions, and cook over a low heat until the onions are lightly cooked but not browned. Add the potatoes and stir until well mixed. Add salt to taste, and lastly the tamarind water, and bring to the boil. Cover and simmer for 10–12 minutes, or until the potatoes are cooked. If you find that the potatoes are not cooked, add a little water and continue simmering. The finished dish should not have any liquid.

MALU CUTLIS

(FISH BALLS)

A party favourite from Sri Lanka which goes well with cocktails.

MAKES ABOUT 20

1 × 425g/15oz can of mackerel in brine
225g/8oz potatoes, peeled and boiled
½ small onion, very finely chopped
2 green chillies, finely chopped (optional)
1 tablespoon peeled and grated fresh root ginger
juice of 1 lemon or 2 limes
½ teaspoon freshly ground black pepper
½ teaspoon roasted cumin seeds
salt
1 egg
oil for deep-frying
55g/2oz breadcrumbs

1. Remove the skin and the central bone from the mackerel. Put into a strainer and leave for 15 minutes to allow the liquid to drain away. Put the fish into a bowl and roughly flake it with a fork.
2. Add the potatoes and mash together with the fish. Add the onion, chillies, ginger, lemon or lime juice, pepper, cumin and salt to taste and mix thoroughly. Make into ball shapes, roughly the size of ping-pong balls. (You should have about 20.) Place the fish balls on a tray, cover with clingfilm, and refrigerate for 30 minutes.
3. Beat the egg in a shallow bowl. Put the oil to heat over a medium flame. Dip each fish ball into the beaten egg. Coat in breadcrumbs and put into the hot oil. I usually fry about 5 at a time but this depends on the size of the pan. The oil should be fairly hot, and the fish balls take only about 3–4 minutes to brown. Drain on a cooling rack for 5 minutes before serving.

FISH PATTIES

These savoury mini-pasties, served as snacks at parties in Sri Lanka, are filled with either a spicy meat or fish filling.

MAKES ABOUT 20

For the pastry
225g/8oz plain flour
½ teaspoon baking powder
½ teaspoon salt
55g/2oz butter or margarine
1 small egg, lightly beaten
100ml/3½fl oz cold water

For the filling
1 × 400g/14oz can of tuna in brine
2 tablespoons oil
1 medium onion, finely chopped
10 curry leaves
3 green chillies, finely chopped
2.5cm/1in piece of fresh root ginger, peeled and grated
¼ teaspoon ground turmeric
1 teaspoon ground coriander
1 teaspoon ground cumin
1 teaspoon chilli powder
½ teaspoon ground roasted cumin seeds
225g/8oz potatoes, boiled, peeled and diced
juice of 1 lime
2 tablespoons coconut milk powder
salt
oil for deep-frying

1. To make the pastry: sift the flour into a bowl. Add the baking powder and salt. Rub in the butter or margarine until the mixture resembles fine breadcrumbs.
2. Make a well in the centre of the flour and work in the egg and sufficient water (approximately 4 tablespoons) to mix to a stiff dough. Knead until smooth. Cover the pastry and allow to rest for 30 minutes.
3. Drain the tuna in a sieve.
4. Heat the oil in a heavy-based frying pan. Add the onion and curry leaves, and fry until the onion is very lightly browned. Add the chillies, ginger, turmeric, coriander, cumin, chilli powder and cumin seeds and fry for a couple of seconds. Add the tuna and the potatoes, and stir until well mixed. Add the lime juice, coconut milk powder and salt, and stir. Leave to cool.
5. On a lightly floured surface roll out half the pastry to roughly a 35cm/14in circle. Using a 7.5cm/3in pastry cutter, cut out about 10 circles of pastry. Place a small quantity of the filling in the centre, moisten the edges and seal to resemble a semi-circle. Leave covered until all the pastry is used up.
6. Heat the oil over a low to medium heat. Fry a few patties at a time until golden-brown. Leave to cool on a wire rack. Repeat until all the patties are fried, then repeat steps 1–6 with the remaining half of the pastry.

VADE

(LENTIL RISSOLES)

This is a tasty snack made from ground lentils which are shaped and deep-fried. Though it is made at home, it is essentially bazaar food, made and sold by vendors in places which attract crowds – railway stations, markets and beaches.

SERVES 4

225g/8oz chana dhal
½ medium onion, finely chopped
2 green chillies, chopped
10 curry leaves, broken into small pieces
salt
oil for deep-frying

1. Pick over the lentils and wash them in several changes of cold water. Soak them in cold water for 2 hours.
2. Drain the lentils in a strainer and immediately put into a food processor. Reserve 2 tablespoons of whole lentils. Grind the remainder to a smooth paste.
3. In a bowl, mix together the onion, chillies, curry leaves, whole lentils and salt to taste. Wet your hands, divide the mixture into 16 equal portions and shape into mini-hamburger-type patties. Cover with clingfilm until the oil is ready for frying.
4. Heat the oil over a low heat and fry a few patties at a time for 2–3 minutes on each side until golden-brown. Remember that the lentils are raw and need to be cooked slowly on both sides. Drain on a cooling rack. Serve hot or cold.

ULUNDHU VADE

(LENTIL RISSOLES)

This South Indian snack is always served with a hot tamarind-flavoured coconut chutney. These vades resemble savoury mini-doughnuts and are delicious hot or cold.

MAKES 16

225g/8oz urad dhal (split white lentils)
½ medium-sized onion, finely chopped
12 curry leaves, roughly broken into small pieces
4 dried red chillies, roughly broken into small pieces
1 teaspoon fennel seeds
1 tablespoon peeled and grated fresh root ginger
salt
oil for deep-frying

1. Pick over the lentils and wash them in several changes of cold water. Tip the lentils together with 570ml/1 pint cold water into a large pan and leave to soak for 3 hours.
2. Drain the lentils in a strainer and immediately put into a food processor. Grind to a smooth paste.
3. Put the ground lentils, onion, curry leaves, fennel seeds, ginger and salt to taste into a bowl, and mix thoroughly.
4. Heat the oil over a low to medium flame. Wet the palms of your hands and divide the mixture into 16 equal portions. Shape into balls the size of a golf ball and flatten to resemble a mini-doughnut. Using your little finger, make a hole through the centre of each rissole. Set aside on a lightly oiled tray.
5. Carefully lower a rissole into the hot oil and fry over a low heat for 4 minutes on each side, or until golden-brown. (If you use a large enough pan you could fry 3–4 rissoles at a time.) Drain on a cooling rack before drying on kitchen paper.

DAHI VADE

(LENTIL RISSOLES IN YOGURT)

This is a traditional vegetarian dish where lentil rissoles are marinated in spicy yogurt.

MAKES 16

16 lentil rissoles (see page **184***), made as described in Ulundhu Vade recipe, stages 1–5*
500ml/18fl oz plain yogurt
2 tablespoons oil
½ teaspoon black mustard seeds
3 green chillies, chopped
2.5cm/1in piece of fresh root ginger, peeled and chopped
12 curry leaves
¼ teaspoon ground turmeric
a pinch of asafoetida
salt

1. Immerse the warm lentil rissoles in a large bowl of tepid water. Place a side plate on top to ensure that they remain immersed. Leave to soak for 30 minutes.
2. Take each rissole in the palm of your hand and apply gentle pressure to remove the water, making sure that the rissole doesn't break. Leave the rissoles covered until required.
3. Put the yogurt into a bowl and beat with a wooden spoon until smooth.
4. Heat the oil over a medium heat. Add the mustard seeds, cover and heat until they pop. Add the chillies, ginger, curry leaves, turmeric, asafoetida and salt to taste. Remove from the heat and pour into the beaten yogurt. Stir until well mixed.
5. Put the rissoles into the spiced yogurt and leave for 5 hours before serving.

NOTE: This dish is always served at room temperature.

BATATA VADE

(FRIED SPICED POTATO)

These deep-fried potato snacks are often eaten at tea-time.

MAKES ABOUT 16

400g/14oz potatoes
½ medium onion, finely chopped
3 green chillies, finely chopped
5cm/2in piece of fresh root ginger, peeled and chopped
⅛ teaspoon asafoetida
½ teaspoon mango powder (amchoor)
½ teaspoon ground roasted cumin seeds
salt

For the batter
100g/3½oz gram flour
½ teaspoon bicarbonate of soda
½ teaspoon ground cumin
½ teaspoon ground coriander
salt
150ml/¼ pint cold water
oil for deep-frying

1. Put the potatoes into a saucepan of boiling water and simmer until cooked.
2. Peel and roughly mash the potatoes. Add the onions, chillies, ginger, asafoetida, mango powder, cumin and salt. Mix thoroughly.
3. Divide into 16 equal portions and shape into balls.
4. To make the batter: sieve the flour into a bowl. Add the bicarbonate of soda, cumin, coriander and salt to taste. Mix with the water to form a batter. Beat until smooth.
5. Heat the oil until a droplet of batter dropped into it rises to the surface in a couple of seconds. Dip a few potato balls at a time into the batter to coat thoroughly, and fry over a medium heat until golden-brown. Drain on a cooling rack. Serve hot.

PAKODA

(VEGETABLES IN LENTIL BATTER)

This is a wholesome snack which could be served either with tea or as an accompaniment to a meal.

SERVES 4

1 potato
2 onions
1 green pepper

For the batter
140g/5oz gram flour
½ teaspoon chilli powder
¼ teaspoon ground turmeric
¼ teaspoon baking powder
salt
100ml/3½fl oz water
oil for deep-frying

1. Sieve the flour into a bowl. Add the chilli powder, turmeric, baking powder and salt to taste. Gradually add the water and mix to form a thick batter. Beat until smooth.
2. Heat the oil over a low to medium heat. Peel the potato and onions, core and deseed the green pepper, and cut into bite-sized pieces. Dip a few vegetable pieces at a time into the batter, to coat thoroughly, and deep-fry in the hot oil until golden-brown. Drain on a cooling rack and serve hot.

NOTE: To vary the flavour, finely shredded onions or finely chopped coriander leaves and green chillies, or ½ teaspoon each of ground cumin and coriander, can be added to the batter.

POHA

(SPICY FLAKED RICE)

A popular tea-time snack. Flaked rice, from which this dish is made, is now available in most supermarkets. Poha should be served in small bowls and eaten with a spoon.

SERVES 4

225g/8oz flaked rice
3 tablespoons oil
½ teaspoon black mustard seeds
¼ teaspoon ground turmeric
a pinch of asafoetida
8 curry leaves
140g/5oz potatoes, peeled and diced
5cm/2in piece of fresh root ginger, peeled and finely chopped
1 medium onion, finely chopped
2 green chillies, chopped
8 tablespoons cold water
100g/5oz frozen peas
salt
juice of ½ lemon
30g/1oz coriander leaves, chopped

1. Wash the flaked rice in a sieve and leave to drain.
2. Heat the oil in a medium saucepan. Add the mustard seeds, cover and allow to pop over a low heat. Add the turmeric, asafoetida, the curry leaves, potatoes, ginger, onion and chillies and stir-fry for 3 minutes. Add the water and bring to the boil. Cover, lower the heat and simmer for 5–7 minutes, or until the potatoes are cooked through. Add the peas, the flaked rice and salt to taste, and stir for 2 minutes over a low heat. Cover and allow to cook for a further 2 minutes. Add the lemon juice and the coriander leaves and mix thoroughly. Serve warm.

UPAMA

(SAVOURY SEMOLINA)

This is a South Indian breakfast dish, but is equally nice eaten as a snack or with a curry for a main meal.

SERVES 4

400g/14oz coarse semolina
1 tablespoon oil
1 medium onion, finely chopped
½ teaspoon cumin seeds
¼ teaspoon ground turmeric
1 teaspoon peeled and finely chopped fresh root ginger
a few curry leaves (optional)
2 green chillies (optional)
110g/4oz fresh or frozen peas
2 carrots, grated
2 tomatoes, peeled and chopped
salt
a knob of butter
a handful of cashew nuts

1. Dry-roast the semolina in a heavy-based frying pan over a low heat, stirring constantly to prevent the semolina from burning. The semolina should be roasted until pale brown.
2. Heat the oil in a saucepan and fry the onion until golden-brown. Add the cumin seeds, turmeric, ginger, curry leaves and chillies, if using, and 700ml water. Add the peas, carrots and tomatoes with 24 fl oz water and bring to the boil. Lower the heat and allow to simmer for 10 minutes. Add the roasted semolina and salt to taste, and stir over the lowest possible heat for 3–5 minutes.
3. Remove from the heat, cover and leave for 5 minutes. Add the butter and cashew nuts. Serve with mixed pickle (see page **169**).

NOTE: Coarse semolina is available from Indian supermarkets.

CHICKEN MULLIGATAWNY

This spicy, coconut-flavoured South Indian soup is eaten in Sri Lanka with string hoppers or rice sticks (see page **57**). It can also be served as a first course.

SERVES 4

For the stock
450g/1lb chicken pieces
1 litre/1¾ pints water
3 ripe tomatoes
2.5cm/1in piece of fresh root ginger, peeled
2.5cm/1in piece of screwpine (optional)
¼ teaspoon ground turmeric
½ teaspoon chilli powder
2 medium onions, chopped
4 cloves of garlic, chopped
2.5cm/1in cinnamon stick
10 curry leaves
10 black peppercorns
salt

For the spicing
2 tablespoons coriander seeds
1½ teaspoons cumin seeds
½ teaspoon fennel seeds
3 tablespoons coconut milk powder
juice of 1 lime

For the seasoning
1 tablespoon oil
½ medium onion, finely chopped
½ teaspoon fennel seeds
5 curry leaves

1. To make the stock: combine all the stock ingredients in a large saucepan. Bring to the boil and simmer, covered, for 1 hour. Strain the stock. Remove the chicken meat from the bones and put into the stock, discarding the bones. Cool the stock and skim off the surface fat.
2. To prepare the spicing: dry-roast the coriander, cumin and fennel seeds in a heavy-based frying pan until they become a little darker. Grind to a fine powder (see page **20**).
3. Bring the stock back to the boil. Add the coconut milk powder, lime juice and ground spices. Simmer over a very low heat while you prepare the seasoning.
4. Heat the oil in a small saucepan over a low heat. Add the onion, fennel seeds and curry leaves and fry until the onion is golden-brown. Pour the mixture into the simmering soup. Serve hot.

DEVILLED CASHEW NUTS

Served with drinks, devilled cashew nuts are a must at Sri Lankan parties. Packaged devilled cashew nuts are available at cinemas and theatres and are eaten as snacks.

SERVES 4

oil for deep-frying
225g/8oz cashew nuts
salt
½ teaspoon chilli powder

1. Heat the oil over a low to medium heat. Do not let it reach smoking point.
2. Add the cashew nuts and keep turning them over constantly in the oil until they become pale brown. Remove from the heat quickly and drain on kitchen paper.
3. Sprinkle with salt and chilli powder while lukewarm. Allow to get cold, then store in an airtight jar.

NOTE: The temperature of the oil is critical – if it is too hot, the cashew nuts will burn. They should be removed from the heat when they are barely brown. If overcooked they will taste bitter.

DESSERTS AND SWEET DRINKS

MANGO MOUSSE

This is a recipe I created for the Cordon Bleu/*Independent* cookery competition. It is a deliciously light, easy-to-make sweet which never fails to please.

SERVES 6

1 × 400g/14oz can evaporated milk
150ml/¼ pint cold water
3 teaspoons powdered gelatine
2 tablespoons caster sugar
1 × 850g/1lb 14oz can mango pulp or 10 fresh mangoes (see Note below)

1. Place the can of evaporated milk in a saucepan with boiling water to cover and simmer for 20 minutes, making sure that the water is topped up so that the can remains immersed in water. Cool the tin and freeze overnight.
2. Put the water into a small saucepan. Sprinkle on the gelatine and leave for 5 minutes to sponge. Melt over a very low heat without boiling until dissolved.
3. Open the can of frozen evaporated milk and tip the contents into a large bowl. Roughly chop into pieces so that the milk can be whisked easily. Using an electric beater, whisk the milk until light and frothy. Add the sugar and the mango pulp and continue to whisk until well mixed. Add the liquid gelatine, mix well and pour into a glass bowl. Refrigerate for 3 hours, until set.

NOTE: If fresh mangoes are used, peel them and remove the stones. Place in a blender with 95g/3oz sugar and the juice of 1 lime and blend until smooth.

MANGO ICE CREAM

Mango ice cream made in a traditional Indian way without eggs or cream is a refreshing finale to any spicy meal.

SERVES 6–8

3.4 litres/6 pints full-fat milk
6 tablespoons icing sugar
1 × 850g/1lb 14oz can mango pulp (see previous recipe)

1. Begin by chilling a 2 litre/3½ pint plastic container in the freezer.
2. Place the milk in a large, heavy-based saucepan and bring to the boil. Keep the milk over a medium to low heat and stir occasionally. After an hour the milk should be stirred constantly to prevent it from sticking to the pan. It takes about 2 hours of boiling down for the milk to reach the consistency of evaporated milk. There should be one-quarter of the original amount of milk. Allow the milk to get cold in a refrigerator.
3. Place the cold milk in a large bowl, and, using an electric hand whisk, beat for 1 minute. Add the sugar and the mango pulp and heat for a further minute, until well mixed. Pour into the cold container, and freeze for 2 hours.
4. Remove from the freezer and beat the partially set ice cream. Put back into the freezer and after 2 hours repeat the whisking process. Re-chill until frozen.

NOTES: The best mango pulp on the market is Kissan Alphonso. Canned mango pulp is sweetened so this ice cream needs very little extra sugar.

For a shorter version of this recipe, 2 × 400g/14oz cans of evaporated milk could be used, as in the Kulfi recipe (see page **197**), instead of reducing the fresh milk.

KULFI

(ICE CREAM)

Kulfi, Indian ice cream, is made by slowly boiling down a large quantity of milk. The reduced milk is flavoured before being frozen in conical metal containers. Since boiling down milk is rather time-consuming you can make Kulfi with canned evaporated milk, although the result is less authentic.

SERVES 3–4

2 × 400g/14oz cans of evaporated milk
6 cardamom pods
5 tablespoons caster sugar
½ teaspoon almond essence
3 tablespoons ground almonds
¼ teaspoon cardamom seeds, crushed

To decorate
110g/4oz unsalted pistachio nuts, chopped

1. Begin by chilling a 1 litre/1¾ pint plastic container in the freezer.
2. Put the evaporated milk and cardamom pods into a heavy-based saucepan and bring slowly to the boil. Leave the pan over a low heat, stirring continuously to prevent the milk from sticking to the pan, for about 10 minutes, when the milk will have reduced sufficiently to proceed to the next stage. Remove from the heat and discard the cardamom pods.
3. Add the sugar to the milk and stir until dissolved. Allow the milk to cool. Add the almond essence, the ground almonds and the crushed cardamom seeds. Place this mixture in the cold container and freeze for 2 hours. Remove from the freezer and, using an electric hand whisk, beat for 1 minute. Put back into the freezer, and after 2 hours repeat the process. Freeze again until frozen. If you do not have an electric whisk, merely stirring the mixture vigorously is sufficient to prevent ice crystals from forming.
4. An hour before serving transfer the ice cream from the freezer to the fridge. Decorate with pistachio nuts.

NOTE: Using fresh milk, place 3.4 litres/6 pints full-fat milk in a large, heavy-based saucepan and bring to the boil. Keep the milk over a medium to low heat and stir occasionally. After an hour the milk should be stirred constantly to prevent it from sticking to the pan. It takes about 2 hours of boiling down for the milk to reach the consistency of evaporated milk. There should be one-quarter of the original amount of milk. Now proceed as with evaporated milk above.

TROPICAL FRUIT SALAD

A fruit salad served with ice cream is one of the most popular Sri Lankan desserts. Although sugar is always added to a fruit salad in Sri Lanka, I usually leave it out, particularly as tropical fruits are naturally sweet. As children, we used to hover around the kitchen when a fruit salad was being made to nibble round the mango stone and to chew on the core of the pineapple.

SERVES 6–8

2 passion-fruits
3 tablespoons boiling water
1 large papaya
2 mangoes
1 pineapple
2 bananas
juice of 1 lime
55g/2oz caster sugar (optional)

1. Cut the passion-fruits in half. Scoop out the flesh and put it into a bowl. Add the water. Put through a sieve and extract as much of the fruit as possible by pressing down with the back of a metal spoon. Discard the seeds and reserve the strained passion-fruit pulp and juice.
2. Cut the papaya in half and peel the halves. Remove the seeds and scrape away any fibres left on the flesh near the seeds. Cut the flesh into 2.5cm/1in cubes.
3. Peel the mangoes. Cut 2 slices from each side of the mangoes, keeping as close to the stone as possible. Then cut into 2.5 cm/1 in pieces.
4. Using a sharp knife, cut off the pineapple skin. Cut the pineapple in half lengthwise. Cut each half into 4 strips. Cut off the central core and discard. Cut each strip into 2.5cm/1in pieces.
5. Peel and slice the bananas. Sprinkle the lime juice over the bananas.
6. Combine the fruit in a large bowl. Sprinkle with the sugar, if using, and mix carefully, so that the pieces of fruit do not get damaged. Cover with clingfilm and refrigerate for 2 hours. Serve with ice cream.

NOTES: When buying passion-fruit, note that if the outer skin is somewhat shrivelled, the fruit is ripe!

In Sri Lanka we don't usually eat the passion-fruit seeds.

SRI LANKAN SEMOLINA PUDDING

Semolina puddings have a reputation for being stodgy and unappealing. This subtly flavoured version has converted many a reluctant taker.

SERVES 4

30g/1oz semolina
30g/1oz butter
425ml/¾ pint milk
55g/2oz caster sugar
30g/1oz cashew nuts, chopped
30g/1oz sultanas
2 tablespoons rosewater
⅛ teaspoon freshly grated nutmeg

1. Fry the semolina in the butter in a heavy-based saucepan over a low heat for about 5 minutes, stirring constantly to prevent the semolina from burning. Add the milk and sugar and bring slowly to the boil. Lower the heat to a simmer and continue to stir for about 10–15 minutes until the semolina is thick. Add the nuts, sultanas, the rosewater and nutmeg. Stir until well mixed. Serve hot or cold.

SAGO PUDDING

Sago is the granulated starch extracted from the seeds of certain palms (mainly *Metroxylon sagu*). It makes an ideal hot-weather dessert as it is cooling in the yin-yang sense: it is an Eastern belief that all foods have both cooling and warming properties in varying proportions, but some – for example yogurt, sago and mung beans – are predominantly cooling, and others – such as squid, tuna and chocolate – are predominantly warming. For healthy eating, meals would be planned to strike a complementary balance between the two properties; for example when eating squid either stuff it with mung beans or eat yogurt for dessert. This food philosophy resembles the wider concepts of yin-yang. In Chinese thought these are the complementary forces that comprise all aspects of life.

SERVES 4

55g/2oz sago
290ml/½ pint cold water
290ml/½ pint semi-skimmed milk
85g/3oz granulated sugar
55g/2oz creamed coconut
¼ teaspoon freshly grated nutmeg
1 teaspoon vanilla essence

1. Wash the sago in several changes of water, then soak in the 290ml/½ pint of cold water for 30 minutes.
2. Put the sago, soaking water, milk and sugar into a heavy-based saucepan and bring slowly to the boil. Add the creamed coconut and continue to cook over a low heat, stirring continually until the coconut has dissolved. Simmer for a further 15 minutes over a very low heat, stirring to prevent the sago from sticking to the pan. Add the nutmeg and vanilla and simmer for a further 5 minutes. Pour into 4 serving glasses and chill for 30 minutes.

NOTE: Sago is all too often confused with tapioca. Though the two are similar in texture and appearance, they have different origins, tapioca being the starch extracted from the root of the cassava plant.

SHEMAI

(VERMICELLI PUDDING)

This is a Bangladeshi version of Payasam (see page **202**). The fine vermicelli required is available from Indian shops. Because of the high fat content, this dish should be served at room temperature, not chilled.

SERVES 6–8

500ml/18fl oz water
4 cardamom pods
3 bay leaves
7.5cm/3in cinnamon stick
55g/2oz ghee (see page **32***) or unsalted butter*
110g/4oz fine vermicelli, broken into 5cm/2in pieces
100g/3½oz caster sugar
55g/2oz cashew nuts, chopped
55g/2oz sultanas

To decorate
1 tablespoon desiccated coconut

1. Put the water into a medium saucepan and add the cardamom, bay leaves and cinnamon. Bring slowly to the boil. Simmer for 5 minutes.
2. Meanwhile, melt the ghee or butter in a heavy-based saucepan over a low to medium heat. Add the vermicelli and fry until it is dark brown. Since the vermicelli is fine, care must be taken not to burn it. Now strain the water in which the spices have been simmering into the pan with the vermicelli, discarding the spices and the bay leaves. Add the sugar and cook over a low heat until the liquid has evaporated. Add the nuts and sultanas, and mix thoroughly. Put into a serving dish and sprinkle with the coconut. Serve at room temperature.

PAYASAM

(VERMICELLI MILK PUDDING)

This delicately flavoured vermicelli dessert is popular throughout India. The fine vermicelli required is available in Indian shops. Owing to the fat content, it is best served at room temperature.

SERVES 4

55g/2oz roasted vermicelli
6 cardamoms
55g/2oz ghee (see page **32***) or unsalted butter*
1.5 litres/2½ pints semi-skimmed milk
7 tablespoons sugar
30g/1oz blanched almonds, chopped
4 drops almond essence
1 teaspoon saffron powder, dissolved in 2 teaspoons boiling water

1. Break the vermicelli into 2.5cm/1in strands. Using a mortar and pestle, crush the cardamom seeds.
2. Melt the ghee or butter in a heavy-based saucepan over a low heat. Add the vermicelli and fry until lightly browned. As the vermicelli is very fine and burns easily, the frying should be done over a low to medium heat and the pan should be stirred constantly. Add the milk and sugar and bring to the boil. Keep on a rolling boil for 10 minutes, stirring from time to time. Lower the heat and simmer for 30 minutes, stirring constantly to prevent the vermicelli from sticking to the pan. When the mixture resembles the consistency of porridge, add the almonds, almond essence, saffron and cardamom. Cook for a further 3 minutes.
3. Pour into a serving dish and stir until cold to prevent a skin from forming on the top.

MEETHA PULAO

(SWEET RICE)

A sweet rice dish, delicately flavoured with saffron and spices. It can be eaten in small quantities as a dessert, or as part of any meal.

SERVES 4

100g/3½oz basmati rice
50g/2oz ghee (see page **32***) or unsalted butter*
4 cloves
3 cardamom pods
5cm/2in cinnamon stick
5 tablespoons soft light brown sugar
½ teaspoon saffron powder, dissolved in 2 teaspoons hot water
1 litre/1¾ pints whole milk
55g/2oz sultanas
55g/2oz slivered almonds
1 tablespoon rosewater

1. Wash the rice in a sieve under cold running water until the water runs clear. Allow to drain thoroughly.
2. Heat half the ghee or butter in a medium saucepan. Add the cloves, cardamoms and cinnamon and fry for 30 seconds. Now add the drained rice and fry for 2 minutes. Add the sugar, saffron liquid and milk and bring to the boil. Give the rice a stir, and simmer uncovered for 35 minutes stirring constantly.
3. Heat the remaining ghee or butter in a small frying pan. Add the sultanas and fry for 30 seconds until they plump up. Remove from the pan, add the almonds and fry until lightly browned.
4. Once the rice is cooked, stir in the sultanas and the almonds. Add the rosewater and stir until well mixed. Allow to rest for 10 minutes before serving.

MUNG PAYASAM

(MUNG BEAN PUDDING)

A South Indian milk pudding made from whole mung beans which are cooked in coconut milk. It is traditionally sweetened with jaggery (see page **12**), but I find that soft brown sugar tastes almost as good.

SERVES 6

200g/7oz whole green mung beans
1.1 litres/2 pints water
5 tablespoons coconut milk powder
100g/3½oz soft dark brown sugar
5 cardamom pods
55g/2oz cashew nuts, chopped
30g/1oz sultanas

1. Pick over the mung beans. Wash them in a strainer and leave to drain for 5 minutes. Spread the beans on a clean tea-towel and allow to dry.
2. Dry-roast the beans in a wide, heavy-based pan over a low to medium heat for 12 minutes. Shake the pan from time to time to ensure that the beans roast evenly. The success of this pudding depends on the even roasting of the beans.
3. Put the beans and the water into a medium saucepan and bring to the boil. Cover and simmer for about 1 hour until the beans are soft and there is only very little liquid left. Add the coconut milk powder and the sugar, and stir until the sugar has dissolved. Remove the cardamom seeds from the pods, and using a mortar and pestle crush the seeds. Finally, add the cashew nuts, sultanas and cardamom and stir until well mixed. Remove from the heat and allow to get cold before serving.

WATALAPPAN

(STEAMED COCONUT MILK PUDDING)

This is a Sri Lankan interpretation of a steamed egg custard. It is considered to be the king of puddings, and was served to Queen Elizabeth II on one of her visits! Use only Sri Lankan Kittul jaggery.

SERVES 6

225g/8oz jaggery
100 ml/3.5 fl oz water
150g/5oz creamed coconut
5 eggs
1 teaspoon freshly grated nutmeg

1. Place the jaggery in a pan with half the water. Bring to the boil, then lower the heat and simmer until the jaggery has dissolved. Dissolve the creamed coconut in the remaining water and allow to cool. Beat the eggs and strain into a 1.1 litre/2 pint bowl. Mix the jaggery and milk into the beaten eggs. Add the nutmeg.
2. Cover the bowl with greaseproof paper. Steam in a steamer or colander set over a covered pan of simmering water for 1 hour.
3. Allow to cool, then refrigerate before turning out and serving chilled.

NOTE: The custard can be made in individual ramekin dishes, steamed for 20 minutes.

KIRI PANI

(YOGURT AND TREACLE)

This is the most traditional of Sri Lankan desserts. The buffalo-milk yogurt, which is set in earthenware pots, has a delicious layer of cream. It is always eaten with treacle (*kitul pani*) which can be made by boiling down jaggery (see page **12**), available from Sri Lankan shops. Greek yogurt made from ewe's milk is an excellent substitute for buffalo-milk yogurt and soft dark brown sugar can be used instead of jaggery.

SERVES 4

225g/8oz jaggery
½ cup water
2 × 200g/7oz cartons of Greek yogurt

1. Bring the jaggery and water slowly to the boil in a heavy-based saucepan. The heat should be kept to a minimum until the jaggery has dissolved. Then bring it to the boil and allow to reduce until you have a thick pouring sauce. Strain into a sauce-boat or jug and pour over the yogurt before serving.

SRIKHAND

(SWEETENED YOGURT DESSERT)

This dessert is traditionally made by separating the milk solids in yogurt from the whey. It is a very laborious process which involves straining the yogurt through a piece of muslin. However, I have found that by combining curd cheese and yogurt an equally delicious result can be obtained with very little effort.

SERVES 3–4

225g/8oz curd cheese
3 tablespoons caster sugar
4 tablespoons low-fat bio yogurt
seeds of 4 cardamom pods, crushed
½ teaspoon saffron powder, dissolved in 2 teaspoons boiling water

To decorate
a few roasted flaked almonds

1. In a bowl, beat the curd cheese and the sugar. Add the yogurt, cardamom and saffron liquid, and beat until well mixed. Divide among 4 bowls, cover and chill for 1 hour. Decorate with almonds before serving.

JALEBI

Though deep-fried, these crispy spirals of dough taste surprisingly light and are easy to eat to excess!

MAKES ABOUT 20

200g/7oz strong white flour
a pinch of salt
½ sachet easy-blend dried yeast
4 tablespoons plain low-fat yogurt
200ml/7fl oz tepid water
1 teaspoon saffron powder, dissolved in 1 teaspoon hot water
300ml/½ pint cold water
225g/8oz granulated sugar
oil for deep-frying

1. Mix the flour, the salt and yeast together in a bowl. Add the yogurt, the tepid water and the saffron liquid and beat until smooth. Cover and leave in a warm place until the dough has doubled in size. Beat again.
2. Bring the cold water and sugar slowly to the boil in a medium saucepan until the sugar has dissolved completely. Now increase the heat and boil rapidly for 6–8 minutes. Remove from the heat and allow to get cold.
3. Heat the oil over a medium heat. Using an icing bag fitted with a nozzle no bigger than 4mm/⅙in, pipe spirals of dough into the hot oil. The spirals of dough should measure about 7cm/2¾in in diameter, with about 4–5 turns of the spiral. I find it easier to form the spirals starting from the outermost circle working inwards to the centre. Fry one or two at a time, turning them over so that both sides are crisp and golden-brown. Drain on a cooling rack for 3 minutes. Put the cooled jalebis into the sugar syrup, making sure that they are completely immersed for 2 minutes. Remove from the syrup and place on a plate to allow the excess to drain off. Continue until all the dough is used up.

RAS GULLA

(CHEESE BALLS IN SYRUP)

This traditional Indian sweet is made from milk solids which are shaped and boiled in a sugar syrup. Together with gulab jamuns (see page **211**), they are the most popular of Indian sweets.

SERVES 4

1.1 litres/2 pints whole milk
juice of 2 lemons
800g/1¾lb granulated sugar
290ml/½ pint water
2 tablespoons rosewater

1. Bring the milk to the boil in a large saucepan. Add the lemon juice and continue boiling for 3 minutes. Pour the mixture through a piece of muslin so that the solids will remain and the whey will flow through. Run cold water through the muslin, to wash out the lemon juice from the milk solids. Squeeze as much water as possible from the milk solids, and leave to drain over a pan for 1 hour.

2. On a clean surface knead the milk solids, a little at a time, until smooth, making sure that they bind together. Divide into 12 equal pieces and shape into balls. It is important that there should be no air pockets or surface cracks in the Ras Gullas.

3. Bring the sugar and water to the boil in a medium heavy-based saucepan over a low heat, stirring until the sugar has dissolved. Once the syrup has come to the boil, simmer for 5 minutes. Now put half of the syrup into a bowl and leave to get cold.

4. Bring the remaining syrup back to the boil, then lower the heat so that it is barely simmering. Add the Ras Gullas and cook for 45 minutes. They will rise to the surface and swell up as they absorb the syrup. It is necessary to ensure that the heat is very low or else the Ras Gullas will break. Using a dessertspoon, turn the Ras Gullas over during cooking time to prevent the top side from drying out. Carefully remove the Ras Gullas from the simmering syrup and immediately plunge into the cold syrup. Leave the Ras Gullas covered. They should be kept at room temperature until they are served.

AVOCADO MOUSSE

This recipe was inspired by an avocado mousse that I ate on an Air Lanka flight from London to Colombo. In Sri Lanka avocados are rarely used in a salad or in a salsa, but are mostly eaten as a dessert with grated jaggery or with sweetened condensed milk. Avocados are ripe when they yield slightly to the touch.

SERVES 4

3 ripe medium-sized Hass avocados
2 tablespoons lemon juice
100g/3½oz caster sugar
150g/6oz fromage frais

1. Wash the avocados and halve each lengthwise. Remove the stone and scoop out the flesh with a spoon, making sure you include the dark green flesh nearest the skin.
2. Place the avocados in a food processor together with the lemon juice, sugar and fromage frais. Blend for a minute until smooth and well mixed.
3. Put into a bowl, cover and chill in the refrigerator for 2 hours.

NOTE: Since avocados discolour when exposed to air, it is important to cover securely with clingfilm. Avocado pulp can be made into a delicious ice-cream by substituting sweetened avocado pulp for the mango pulp in the recipe for mango ice-cream on page **196**.

GULAB JAMUN

These rose-flavoured milk balls in syrup are one of the sweets often served on special occasions. They take a little time to make but are well worth the effort.

SERVES 6

1.1 litres/2 pints whole milk
juice of 2 lemons
5 cardamom pods
55g/2oz unsalted butter, softened
55g/2oz skimmed milk powder
55g/2oz self-raising flour
ghee (see page **32***) or oil for deep-frying*
310g/10oz granulated sugar
400ml/14fl oz water
2 tablespoons rosewater

1. Bring the milk to the boil in a large saucepan. Add the lemon juice and continue boiling for 3 minutes. Pour the mixture through a piece of muslin, so that the solids will remain and the whey will flow through. Run cold water through the muslin, to wash out the lemon juice from the milk solids. Squeeze as much of the water as possible from the milk solids and leave to drain over a pan for 1 hour.
2. Remove the seeds from the cardamom pods. Using a mortar and pestle, crush the cardamom seeds.
3. Using the heel of your hand, knead the milk solids, a little at a time, until smooth. Add the butter, milk powder, flour and cardamom seeds. Knead thoroughly. Divide this mixture into 16 equal pieces. Using the palms of your hands, shape each portion into a ball. It is important that there should be no air pockets or surface cracks, or else the balls will burst open during frying. Leave the balls covered with a damp cloth.
4. Heat the ghee or oil over a low heat. Place about 6 balls at a time into the hot oil. They will swell slightly in the oil. The frying has to be done over a low heat and the gulab jamuns should be turned over carefully to ensure that they are uniformly browned and cooked in the centre. Gulab jamuns are normally dark brown in colour. Cool on a wire rack, then drain on kitchen paper.
5. While you are frying the gulab jamuns, bring the sugar and water slowly to the boil in a heavy-based saucepan, and simmer over a low heat until all the sugar has dissolved. Add the rosewater. Remove from the heat and put the warm gulab jamuns into the syrup. Leave for 3–4 hours before serving. The gulab jamuns should be turned over in the cooling syrup so that their surfaces absorb it uniformly.

BANANA FRITTERS

Bananas are abundant in Sri Lanka, and this is a very tasty way of serving them. Unlike their Chinese counterparts, these fritters are not meant to be crisp, but should be soft and succulent.

SERVES 6

100g/3½oz plain flour
pinch of salt
8 tablespoons tepid water
1 tablespoon melted butter
2 egg whites
6 ripe bananas
oil for deep-frying

1. Sift the flour and salt into a bowl, and mix with the water and butter to a thick smooth batter. Whisk the egg whites until stiff. Fold into the flour mixture. Peel each banana and cut in half lengthwise, then cut each piece in half crossways.
2. Heat the oil until smoking-hot. Coat each piece of banana in the batter and fry in the oil until golden-brown. Drain on a cooling rack, and serve hot with a jam sauce.

NOTE: For pineapple fritters, use pineapple rings in place of banana quarters.

LASSI

(SWEETENED YOGURT DRINK)

A refreshing drink for a hot summer's day.

SERVES 4

290ml/½ pint plain yogurt
200ml/7fl oz cold water
2 tablespoons sugar
1 teaspoon rosewater
ice cubes

1. In a blender or food processor blend together the yogurt and the water. Add the sugar and the rosewater and blend for 1 further minute. Serve in tall glasses with ice.

ICE KOPI

(ICED COFFEE)

This can be served in a tall glass with a scoop of ice cream as a delicious summer beverage.

SERVES 6

4 tablespoons instant coffee
1 litre/1¾ pints boiling water
1 × 400g/14oz can sweetened condensed milk
2 tablespoons brandy (optional)
2 teaspoons vanilla essence
425ml/¾ pint cold milk

1. Dissolve the coffee with the water in a large coffee pot. Add the condensed milk and stir until well mixed. Add the brandy, vanilla and milk and pour into bottles. Allow to cool, then refrigerate until well chilled.

PASSION-FRUIT JUICE

When passion-fruits were in season my mother made a concentrated juice which she froze in ice trays. We used to dissolve 2 cubes in a glass of water to make a delicious and refreshing drink. Most food stores and supermarkets in Sri Lanka sell bottles of passion-fruit cordial. Diluted with water this makes a very popular soft drink.

SERVES 4

8 passion-fruits
2–3 tablespoons boiling water
caster sugar to taste
500ml/18fl oz cold water

1. Wash the passion-fruits. Cut each fruit in half crosswise and scoop out the flesh and seeds. Put the flesh and seeds into a bowl, add 2 tablespoons boiling water, and mix thoroughly.
2. Put the passion-fruit pulp and seeds into a sieve and force the pulp through the sieve, using the back of a metal spoon. If you haven't managed to extract all the juice from the seeds and pulp at the first pressing, add another tablespoon of boiling water and repeat the process. Only the bare seeds should remain in the sieve.
3. Add sugar to the strained juice. Dilute with the cold water. Pour into 4 glasses and serve topped up with ice cubes.

NOTE: When left to stand, passion-fruit juice must be stirred before drinking because the fruit pulp settles at the bottom of the glass.

CAKES AND SWEETS

SRI LANKAN CHRISTMAS CAKE

This cake combines traditional ingredients with exotic fruits and spices. In Sri Lanka, a marzipan made of ground cashew nuts is the only icing used, and the cake is served in small pieces which are individually wrapped in decorative paper. Eating this cake was the gastronomic highlight of my year and I used to sneak into the kitchen and taste it during its preparation. Using a food processor to chop the fruit and nuts tends to alter the texture of the cake, and although it is time-consuming, I would advise you to chop all the ingredients by hand.

MAKES 2 CAKES

55g/2oz candied peel
100g/3½oz chow, drained
100g/3½oz stem ginger, drained
100g/3½oz raisins
310g/10oz sultanas
110g/4oz currants
225g/8oz candied ash pumpkin or crystallized pineapple
225g/8oz cashew nuts, chopped
55g/2oz almonds, chopped
100g/3½oz glacé cherries
3 tablespoons brandy
3 tablespoons triple strength rosewater
2 tablespoons clear honey
1 tablespoon vanilla essence
½ nutmeg, freshly grated
2 teaspoons ground cinnamon
1 teaspoon ground cardamom
½ teaspoon ground cloves
oil for greasing
225g/8oz semolina
225g/8oz butter at room temperature
12 eggs
400g/14oz soft light brown sugar

To finish
4 tablespoons brandy

1. Finely chop the preserved fruit and nuts. Put into a bowl together with the brandy, rosewater, honey, vanilla, nutmeg, cinnamon, cardamom and cloves. Mix thoroughly and leave, covered, for 24 hours.
2. Double-line 2 × 20cm/8in cake tins with lightly oiled greaseproof paper. Preheat the oven to 140°C/275°F/gas mark 1.
3. Mix together the semolina and butter in a medium bowl. Separate the eggs. In a large bowl, beat the egg yolks together with the sugar until pale. Mix in the semolina. Add the fruit mixture, a little at a time, using a cutting motion, to make sure that the cake mixture is thoroughly mixed in with the fruit. This

movement provides a lot of wrist exercise!

4. Whisk half the egg whites until stiff. (The rest can be used for meringues.) Add 4 tablespoons of the egg white to the cake mixture and beat it in to slacken it. Fold in the remaining egg whites lightly but thoroughly.

5. Put the cake mixture into the prepared tins and bake in the preheated oven for about 1½ hours, or until a skewer inserted comes out clean. Cool the cakes on a wire rack.

6. Once cold, prick the surfaces with a skewer and pour 2 tablespoons of brandy over each cake. Cover with foil, place in an airtight tin and leave for a week before icing.

NOTE: Triple-strength rosewater is available from chemists' shops.

BIBIKKAN

(SPICY COCONUT CAKE)

The Portuguese probably introduced a cake of this name to both Sri Lanka and Goa, but except for sharing a coconut flavour, the two cakes are quite different. Palm treacle is sold in cans in Sri Lankan shops.

SERVES 8

290ml/½ pint palm treacle
2 tablespoons dark muscovado sugar
170g/6oz desiccated coconut
½ teaspoon ground cinnamon
½ teaspoon ground cardamom
a pinch of ground cloves
butter for greasing
225g/8oz plain flour
½ teaspoon bicarbonate of soda
85g/3oz butter or margarine
3 tablespoons coconut milk powder
55g/2oz cashew nuts, chopped
55g/2oz raisins
7 tablespoons milk
1 teaspoon vanilla essence

1. In a heavy-based saucepan, bring the treacle and sugar slowly to the boil over a low heat. Add the desiccated coconut and cook for 1 minute, then add the cinnamon, cardamom and cloves. Remove from the heat and leave to cool.
2. Preheat the oven to 150°C/300°F/gas mark 2. Grease and line a 25 × 15cm/10 × 6in dish.
3. Sift the flour into a bowl. Add the bicarbonate of soda. Rub in the butter or margarine until the mixture resembles fine breadcrumbs. Add the coconut milk powder, cashew nuts and raisins. Now add the cooled coconut mixture and stir until well mixed. Lastly add the milk and vanilla. Put into the baking dish and bake for nearly 2 hours or until a skewer inserted into the centre comes out clean. Allow to cool in the dish, then cut into 5cm/2in squares.

COCONUT CAKE

This popular Sri Lankan cake is crusty on top and moist inside.

SERVES 6–8

butter for greasing
4 eggs, separated
225g/8oz caster sugar
225g/8oz desiccated coconut
100g/3½oz ground rice
110g/4oz cashew nuts, chopped
4 tablespoons rosewater
⅛ teaspoon ground cardamom
¼ teaspoon ground cinnamon
pinch of ground cloves

1. Grease and line a 27.5 × 17.5cm/ 11 × 7in cake tin. Preheat the oven to 170°C/325°F/gas mark 3.
2. Whisk the egg yolks and sugar until thick and creamy. Add the coconut and fold in the ground rice. Add the cashew nuts, rosewater, cardamom, cinnamon and cloves. Whisk the egg whites until stiff, and fold into the cake mixture.
3. Put into the cake tin and bake in the centre of the preheated oven for 45 minutes. Cool in the tin for 10 minutes before turning out on to a cooling rack.

SRI LANKAN LOVE CAKE

Cake is not indigenous to Sri Lanka, but is one of the many influences left behind by colonization. This rich and unusual cake combines the tradition of European cake-making with the exotic flavours of the East.

SERVES 16

butter for greasing
225g/8oz semolina
170g/6oz unsalted butter
10 egg yolks
450g/1lb soft light brown sugar
340g/12oz cashew nuts, finely chopped
½ teaspoon freshly grated nutmeg
1 teaspoon ground cinnamon
1 tablespoon rosewater
2 teaspoons vanilla essence
1 teaspoon grated lemon zest
4 egg whites
1 tablespoon clear honey

1. Grease and line 2 30 × 25cm/12 × 10in cake tins. Preheat the oven to 150°C/ 300°F/gas mark 2.
2. Dry-roast the semolina in a heavy-based saucepan over a low heat until lightly browned. Using a palette knife, mix the semolina and the butter, and leave in a warm place.
3. In a large bowl, beat the egg yolks and sugar until light and creamy. Add the semolina and butter mixture, and beat until well mixed. Add the cashew nuts, nutmeg, cinnamon, rosewater, vanilla, and lemon zest, and mix thoroughly. Whisk the egg whites until stiff. Add about 2 tablespoons of the egg whites to the cake mixture and beat. Using a metal spoon, fold in the remaining egg whites.
4. Pour the cake mixture into the tins and bake in the preheated oven for 1 hour, or until a skewer inserted into the centre of the cake comes out clean. Allow to cool in the tin. This cake is usually cut into small squares for serving. It is best eaten one day after it has been baked, and can be stored in an airtight container for up to 2 weeks.

JAGGERY CAKE

This cake contains no flour or baking powder, so the texture is quite different from other cakes. The spices and coconut milk powder give it an unusual flavour. If you cannot buy jaggery easily, substitute dark muscovado sugar.

SERVES 8

225g/8oz semolina
butter for greasing
110g/4oz butter or margarine at room temperature
3 large eggs, separated
170g/6oz soft light brown sugar
1 teaspoon ground cinnamon
¼ teaspoon freshly grated nutmeg
¼ teaspoon ground cardamom
1 teaspoon vanilla essence
2 teaspoons rosewater
110g/4oz cashew nuts, coarsely chopped
85g/3oz jaggery, grated or very finely chopped
4 teaspoons coconut milk powder
2 tablespoons water

1. Dry-roast the semolina in a heavy-based saucepan over a very low heat, for about 15 minutes, stirring constantly to prevent the semolina from burning. Remove from the heat and leave to cool.
2. Grease and line a 23cm/9in cake tin. Preheat the oven to 150°C/300°F/gas mark 2.
3. Using a palette knife, mix the semolina and the butter or margarine. Separate the egg yolks from the whites and put into separate bowls. Using an electric hand whisk, beat the yolks and sugar until light and creamy. Add the semolina and butter mixture, and mix together. Whisk the egg whites until stiff. Add 1 tablespoon of the egg whites to the cake mixture and stir to slacken it. Add the cinnamon, nutmeg, cardamom, vanilla, rosewater, cashew nuts, jaggery and coconut milk powder. Add the water and mix thoroughly. Using a metal spoon, fold in the remaining egg whites.
4. Pour into the tin and bake in the centre of the preheated oven for about 30 minutes, or until a skewer inserted into the centre comes out clean. Cool on a wire rack.

SEMOLINA HALVA

Halva is a sweetmeat and its popularity extends all the way from India to Greece, each nation having its own version. For this particular recipe it is essential to use coarse semolina which is available from Indian shops.

MAKES 24 PIECES

310g/11oz coarse semolina
100g/3½oz ghee (see page **32***) or unsalted butter*
570ml/1 pint milk
170g/6oz sugar
55g/2oz almonds, chopped
1 teaspoon almond essence
½ teaspoon saffron powder, dissolved in 2 teaspoons hot water

1. Dry-roast the semolina in a heavy-based saucepan until pale brown, stirring constantly to prevent it from burning.
2. Lightly grease a 27.5 × 17.5cm/ 11 × 7in tray with a little of the ghee or butter.
3. Add the remaining ghee or butter and the milk and sugar to the semolina in the pan and cook until the mixture is quite stiff and leaves the sides of the pan. Add the almonds, the almond essence and the saffron liquid. Stir until well mixed. Pat the semolina into the tray and leave to become cold, then cut into 2.5cm/1in squares.

CARROT HALVA

This halva is made in every region of India. Because of its high fat content it must be served at room temperature, not chilled.

SERVES 4–6

450g/1lb carrots, finely grated
55g/2oz almonds, chopped
140g/5oz caster sugar
720ml/1¼ pints semi-skimmed milk
6 cardamoms
85g/3oz ghee (see page **32***) or unsalted butter*

To decorate
flaked almonds

1. Put the carrots, almonds, sugar and milk into a heavy-based saucepan and stir over a low heat until the sugar has dissolved. Cook over a medium heat for about 1½ hours, until the mixture thickens and most of the liquid has evaporated. The pan should be stirred from time to time to prevent the carrots from sticking to the bottom, particularly during the latter stages of cooking.
2. Using a mortar and pestle, crush the cardamom seeds. Melt the ghee or butter in a saucepan. Stir in the carrot mixture and fry over a low to medium heat until the carrots become a reddish-brown. Add the cardamom and stir until well mixed. Decorate with the flaked almonds and serve at room temperature in small bowls.

AGAR-AGAR JELLY

Agar-agar, which is a jelly made from seaweed, is odourless and colourless and sets without refrigeration even in the tropics. It is widely used in South-East Asia and in the Far East. My mother used to flavour agar-agar with coconut milk and jaggery. I prefer to flavour it with a fruit purée and once the jelly sets I cut it into cubes and serve it chilled with chopped fruit, rather like the almond jelly served in Chinese restaurants.

SERVES 10–12

15g/½oz agar-agar
1 litre/1¾ pints cold water
850g/29oz Alfonso canned mango pulp
150g/5oz caster sugar

1. Cut the agar-agar strands into 5cm/2in pieces.
2. Soak the agar-agar in the cold water for 8 hours or overnight.
3. Put the agar-agar and the soaking water into a large saucepan and bring slowly to the boil. Stir over a low heat until the strands have dissolved. Increase the heat and boil for 2–3 minutes, continuing to stir to prevent sticking. Add the mango pulp and the sugar and stir until the sugar has dissolved.
4. Rinse 4 shallow rectangular dishes 25 × 15cm/10 × 6in in cold water. Pour in the warm jelly. Leave to set at room temperature.
5. Once set, cover and chill in the refrigerator.
6. Cut the jelly into 2.5cm/1in cubes and pile into a glass serving bowl.

NOTE: Agar-agar is available in Chinese supermarkets. Alfonso mango pulp is available in Indian shops. The weight stated on the agar-agar packets is sometimes incorrect, so check before using.

MASUR PAK

A fudge-like sweet which is very calorific!

MAKES 16 PIECES

140g/5oz gram flour
4 cardamom pods
200g/7oz granulated sugar
200ml/7fl oz water
100g/3½oz ghee (see page **32***), melted*

1. Dry-roast the gram flour in a heavy-based saucepan, over a low to medium heat, for about 20 minutes, stirring constantly to prevent the flour from burning. Sieve the flour and reserve.
2. Using a mortar and pestle, crush the cardamom seeds. Lightly grease a 20cm/8in square baking tin or dish.
3. In another saucepan, dissolve the sugar in the water over a low heat. Once dissolved, bring the syrup to the boil, and allow to boil for 3 minutes.
4. The next stage is rather tricky. You have to combine the flour with the ghee and sugar syrup. Heat the ghee in a small saucepan until melted. Put half the fat together with half the syrup into a medium saucepan, and bring slowly to the boil over a low heat. Add the flour and stir until well mixed. Now add the remaining fat and syrup and stir constantly over a low heat until the mixture leaves the sides of the pan and comes together. Add the cardamom and spread in the tin or dish. Allow to get cold before cutting into squares.

ALMOND BURFI

These traditional Indian sweets are rather time-consuming to make but are well worth the effort. They are delicious! Boxes of Burfi are often presented as gifts, just as boxes of chocolates are in the West.

MAKES 20 PIECES

1.1 litres/2 pints full-fat milk
juice of 1 large lemon
30g/1oz icing sugar for dusting
55g/2oz skimmed milk powder
55g/2oz unsalted butter at room temperature
55g/2oz ground almonds
225g/8oz caster sugar
1½ teaspoons almond essence

1. Grease a 20cm/8in baking tin. Bring the milk to the boil in a large saucepan. Add the lemon juice and continue boiling for 3 minutes. Take a large piece of muslin and strain the milk into a bowl. Squeeze out as much of the whey as possible.
2. On a clean surface lightly dusted with icing sugar, knead the milk solids together with the skimmed milk powder as you would a bread dough for about 5 minutes. Now add the butter, the ground almonds and the caster sugar, and knead for 1 further minute until well mixed.
3. Cook the sweet mixture in a heavy-based saucepan over a low heat, stirring constantly and breaking up the solid particles with the back of the spoon, if necessary, for 20–30 minutes, or until the mixture leaves the sides of the pan. Add the almond essence, mix thoroughly, and pat into the baking tin. Leave to become cold, then cut into 2.5cm/1in squares.

SEMOLINA AND COCONUT ROCK

This Sri Lankan candy is a great favourite with children.

MAKES 16 PIECES

butter for greasing
225g/8oz sugar
4 tablespoons water
140g/5oz semolina
30g/1oz grated or desiccated coconut
½ tablespoon rosewater
1 teaspoon ground cardamom

1. Lightly grease a 20cm/8in square dish.
2. Put the sugar and water into a saucepan and stir over a low heat until the syrup boils. Add the semolina and cook for about 5 minutes. Add the coconut, rosewater and cardamom, and continue to cook, stirring, for about 10 minutes, or until the mixture leaves the sides of the pan. Pour into the dish and allow to get cold, then cut into pieces.

POL TOPI

(COCONUT ROCK)

This rock-hard Sri Lankan candy is popular with children as it is very sweet. The desiccated coconut available in Indian shops is more finely shredded than the supermarket brands.

MAKES 12 PIECES

butter for greasing
200g/7oz sugar
100ml/4fl oz water
100g (3½oz) fine desiccated coconut
3 drops of food colouring (optional)
2–3 drops vanilla essence

1. Lightly grease a 17.5cm/7in square dish.
2. Put the sugar and the water into a saucepan and cook over a low heat until the sugar has dissolved. Bring rapidly to the boil, and continue boiling for 1 minute. Add the coconut and stir over a low heat for about 4–6 minutes, or until the mixture leaves the sides of the pan. Add the colouring and vanilla. Pat the mixture into the dish. Cut into 2.5cm/1in pieces when cold.

KIRI TOPI

(SRI LANKAN MILK TOFFEE FUDGE)

Typically Sri Lankan and very sweet.

MAKES ABOUT 24 PIECES

butter for greasing
400g/14oz can of sweetened condensed milk
½ condensed milk tin of water
200g/7oz sugar
1 heaped teaspoon cocoa powder, dissolved in ½ teaspoon hot water
55g/2oz butter
55g/2oz cashew nuts, chopped

1. Lightly grease a 20cm/8in square dish.
2. Place the condensed milk, water and sugar in a heavy-based pan. Cook over a low heat for about 40 minutes, or until the mixture leaves the sides of the pan and seems slightly dry. Add the cocoa, butter and nuts and cook for a further 5 minutes. Remove from the heat, and pat into the dish. Cut into 2.5cm/1in squares while warm and leave to become cold.

SESAME SWEETS

These sweets are usually made with jaggery, but they taste equally good made with brown sugar.

MAKES 24 PIECES

butter for greasing
225g/8oz unhusked sesame seeds
225g/8oz soft dark brown sugar
100ml/3½fl oz cold water

1. Lightly grease 2 dinner plates with butter. Dry-roast the sesame seeds in a heavy-based frying pan over a low to medium heat for 5–7 minutes.
2. Bring the sugar and water slowly to the boil in a saucepan. Once the sugar has dissolved, add the sesame seeds and continue cooking over a low to medium heat for about 12–15 minutes, until the mixture leaves the sides of the pan and you notice a slight oiliness in the mixture. Put on to the 2 plates and with a spatula pat into a square shape. Cut each into 12 pieces. Allow to become cold before storing in an airtight container.

MENU SUGGESTIONS

As in most other cuisines, there are no set rules in Sri Lanka and India about what should be eaten with what. However, there are a few general eating traditions which vary from region to region over the sub-continent. In North India, it is customary to start a meal by eating some form of unleavened bread with vegetables, which would be followed by rice and dhal. Sweets are eaten alongside this main course. Food is served on a *thali*, a large, circular stainless-steel tray. Small bowls are arranged inside the *thali* for the dishes that contain gravy. It is usual to have a very small mound of salt on the *thali* to use as required.

On festive occasions in South India, food is eaten on banana leaves which serve as disposable plates. In Sri Lanka, the rice platter is placed at the centre of the table, with curries and vegetables arranged around it.

When I am planning a menu, I make sure that it is nutritionally balanced to include rice, lentils, meat or fish, salad and vegetables. I also try to provide a variety of textures, colours and flavours. Listed below are a few of my favourite menu combinations.

Menu 1

Kahabath (page 40)
Ala Thel Dhaala (page 72)
Sri Lankan Chicken Curry (page 142)
Aubergine Curry (page 62)
Pappadams (page 173)
Seeni Sambal (page 166)
Tomato and Onion Salad (page 156)

Menu 2

Chicken Biriyani (page 48)
Undey Ki Kari (page 110)
Curried Fried Okra (page 64)
Cucumber Raita (page 158)
Date Chutney (page 159)

Menu 3

Kichiri (page 43)
Saar (page 111)
Cauliflower Bhaji (page 72)
Pappadams (page 173)
Pickles (page 168–9)

Menu 4

Boiled Rice (page 37)
Beef Curry (page 129)
Parippu (page 99)
Mallung (page 80)
Pol Sambal (page 161)

Menu 5

Dosa with Potato Filling (page 179, 180)
Sambar (page 105)
Green Coriander Coconut Chutney (page 162)

Menu 6

Poori (page 51)
Bhindi Bhaji (page 64)
Curd Rice (page 38)
Pappadams (page 173)

Menu 7

Kofta (page 136)
Vegetable Pulao (page 45)
Chole Chaat (page 102)
Aubergine Curry (page 62)
Bhindi Bhaji (page 64)
Cucumber Raita (page 158)

Menu 8

Indiappam (page 57)
Seeni Sambal (page 166)
Ala Sudhata (page 70)
Jhinga Kari (page 125)

Menu 9

Chapati (page 50)
Bhindi Thoran (page 67)
Boiled Rice (page 37)
Saru (page 100)
Kosemberi (page 155)
Pickles (page 168–9)

Menu 10

Parathas (page 55)
Keema (page 130)
Boiled Rice (page 37)
Dhal Saag (page 103)
Pappadams (page 173)
Radish Salad (page 153)

Menu 11

Boiled Rice (page 37)
Malu Curry (page 117)
Parippu (page 99)
Bean Curry (page 76)
Fried Sprats (page 120)
Tomato and Onion Salad (page 156)

Menu 12

Chapatis (page 50)
Baigan Bharta (page 63)
Masala Rajma (page 108)
Murgh Curry (page 145)
Sabzi Pulao (page 44)
Lettuce with Peanut Dressing (page 157)

Menu 13

Yakhni Pulao (page 42)
Cauliflower and Potato Curry (page 74)
Channa Dhal (page 101)
Lamb Kebab (page 132)
Cucumber Raita (page 158)

Menu 14

Chapatis (page 50)
Dill Bhaji (page 81)
Vegetable Pulao (page 45)
Khatte Lobia (page 107)
Cucumber Raita (page 158)
Pappadams (page 173)

Menu 15

Roti (page 54)
Lunumiris (page 167)
Ambul Thiyal (page 121)

MAIL ORDER ADDRESSES

Specialist Sri Lankan Foodstores

Lihiniya
70 Crickelwood Broadway
London NW2 3EP
Telephone/Fax: 0181 208 2658

Fleet Food and Wine Ltd
197 Edgeware Road
Colindale
London NW9 6LP
Telephone: 0181 205 3804

General Suppliers of Oriental Food

Natco Spices
Lancelot Road
Wembley
Middlesex HA0 2BG
Telephone: 0181 903 7050

Paul's Complete Curry Kitchen
1 Penydarren Drive
Whitchurch
Cardiff CF4 7HT
Telephone: 01222 522195

Curry Direct
P.O. Box 7
Liss Hampshire GU33 7YS
Telephone: 01730 894949

Fox's Spices
Aston Cantlow Road
Wilmcote
Warwickshire CV37 9XN
Telephone: 01789 266420

Fiddes Payne Ltd
The Spice Warehouse
Pepper Alley
Banbury
Oxfordshire OX16 8JB
Telephone: 012295 253888

Wing Yip
395 Edgeware Road
London NW2 6IW
Telephone: 0181 450 0422

INDEX